THE
CHOSEN
ONE

TIGER WOODS
and the dilemma
of greatness

DAVID OWEN

SIMON *&* SCHUSTER
New York • London • Toronto
Sydney • Singapore

SIMON & SCHUSTER
Rockefeller Center
1230 Avenue of the Americas
New York, NY 10020

Designed by Leslie Phillips

For information about special discounts for bulk purchases,
please contact Simon & Schuster Special Sales:
1-800-456-6798 or business@simonandschuster.com

Manufactured in the United States of America

10 9 8 7 6 5 4 3 2 1

Library of Congress Cataloging-in-Publication Data is
available

ISBN 978-1-5011-6972-4

CONTENTS

THE
CHOSEN
ONE

1 OKLAHOMA CITY

TIGER WOODS conducted a golf exhibition in Oklahoma City on a hot Sunday afternoon in May 2000. During the hour before he appeared, while a large crowd baked in the bleachers, a member of his entourage held a trivia contest, with T-shirts for prizes. One of the questions: In what year was Tiger Woods born? The first guess, by a very young fan, was 1925. That's off by half a century, but the error is understandable; Woods has accomplished so much as a golfer that it's easy to forget how young he is. In a sport in which good players seldom peak before their thirties, and often remain competitive at the highest levels well into their forties, Woods is off to a mind-boggling start. He is the youngest player (by two years) to have won all four of modern golf's so-called major tournaments—the Masters, the United States Open, the British Open, and the PGA Championship. He is the only player in history to have won all four in succession. And, as if all that weren't enough, he holds the all-time scoring record in three of them and shares it in the other. After Woods blew out the rest of the field in the 2000 British Open, which he won by eight strokes, Ernie Els, a terrific young South African player and the winner of two U.S. Opens, said with a resigned smile, "We'll have to go to the drawing board again, and maybe make the holes bigger for us and a little smaller for him."

When Woods finally appeared for his Oklahoma exhibition, his entrance was appropriately dramatic. A small convoy of golf carts bore down on the bleachers from the far end of the driving range, while martial-sounding rock music blasted from the public address system. The exhibition was the final event in a two-day program put on by the Tiger Woods Foundation, a charitable organization whose goal is to inspire children—especially underprivileged children—and "to make golf look more like America," as Woods himself says. Forty-two cities had applied for visits by Woods and his team in 2000, and Oklahoma

City was the first of just four cities to be chosen. Among the reasons for its selection was the existence of this particular facility: a low-fee public golf course, with free lessons for children on weekends, situated in an unprepossessing neighborhood not far from Oklahoma City's unprepossessing downtown.

Before stepping up to the practice tee, Woods answered questions from the audience, whose members differed from golf's principal constituency in that many of them were neither middle-aged nor white. One of the first questions came from a junior-high-school-aged fan, who asked, "How do you maintain your personal life and your golf career at the same time?"

Woods, who was leaning on his pitching wedge, said, "That's a great question. When I'm off the golf course, I like to get away from everything, and I like to keep everything private, because I feel that I have a right to that. I have a right to my own private life, and things I like to do." There was heavy applause from the crowd. "But there are exceptions to that, where the press likes to make up a few stories here and there. That's just the way it goes. Sensationalism tends to sell now."

When he said that, I shifted uneasily on the small, roped-off patch of ground from which I and other members of the press had been asked to view the proceedings. Woods doesn't think highly of reporters. Particular journalists have annoyed him repeatedly over the years, and he had a couple of memorably unpleasant experiences early in his career. The best known incident occurred in 1997, when a writer for *GQ* quoted Woods telling off-color jokes and making a variety of indiscreet remarks, all of which Woods had assumed to be off the record. There was nothing truly scandalous about anything that Woods was quoted as saying, and in the long run the writer (whose article is inevitably mentioned in paragraphs like this one) has probably suffered more than his subject has. But the experience was a transforming one for Woods: A certain air of tension—like background radiation—remains detectable in almost all of his media encounters, even though openly chilly exchanges between him and the press have become less frequent as he has resigned himself to the public relations side of his job. (He now knows many of the press tent regulars by name—even by nickname—and he sometimes goes out of his way to be courteous and helpful.) He has always been impatient with people who don't work as hard as he does, and no one in the press tent works as hard as he does. Woods also often seems annoyed that writers who have no contractual business relationship with him are able to profit from his achievements by writing about them. (Sportswriters, for their part, have a tendency to believe that the most telling aspect of any athlete's character is the way in which that athlete treats sportswriters.)

Many very famous people become very famous because, for some compelling and probably unwholesome reason, they crave the approval of the rest of us. That's why they put up with the media, among other things. Even the ones who vigorously defend their privacy do so in a way that attracts an awful lot of publicity, suggesting that their aversion to celebrity is more complicated than they let on. With Woods, though, you get the feeling that his fame mostly gets in his way. We intrude on his golf when he's playing golf, and we intrude on his private life when he's not. He can be a dazzlingly emotional and telegenic performer, and he surely finds it thrilling to walk down fairways lined with thousands of deliriously happy admirers who are shouting his name (or bowing to the ground, as a group of his fans did on the final hole at the 2000 U.S. Open), but he conveys the impression that he would play every bit as hard if the cameras and the microphones and the galleries all went away. His goals are entirely public ones—he wants to be universally recognized as the best in the world, not to exorcise some merely personal demon—but, unlike most celebrities, he shows no sign of needing or desiring or depending on help from any of us.

That's an awe-inspiring character trait, but it's also a chilling one. Part of the fun of being a sports fan is harboring the delusion that great athletic achievements are in a sense collaborations between athletes and their rooting sections. We ourselves may not throw the game-winning touchdown pass, but at some level we believe that our boisterous enthusiasm intimidated the free safety and helped generate the adrenaline that powered the quarterback's arm. Woods's accomplishments are so outsized, though, that it's hard to conceive of them as belonging to anyone but himself. We may cheer him on, but he is clearly measuring his achievements by a standard so high that none of us would have dared to dream it up. The script is his, not ours. As Tom Watson said of him after the 2000 British Open, "He is something supernatural."

Between the mid-1970s and just a year or two ago, sportswriters viewed Jack Nicklaus's remarkable career (which was crowned by eighteen victories in the four major tournaments) as the permanent benchmark of greatness in golf; the new consensus is that Woods has already outdone Nicklaus in several categories, and that eventually he will probably break all of Nicklaus's records unless he loses interest in the game or injures himself or decides to run for President instead. That sportswriters have come to this opinion is no surprise to Woods himself, because he reached the same conclusion back in junior high school: before he turned thirteen, he had researched and memorized Nicklaus's main competitive accomplishments because he already intended to exceed them. He views Nicklaus as the best player in the history of the game, and his goal is, with all due respect, to give the master a run for that title. Nicklaus himself was similarly unabashed in his ambitions as his own career was beginning to unfold. Speaking, in 1960, of Robert Tyre "Bobby" Jones, Jr.—who at that time held the same patriarchal posi-

tion in the golf world that Nicklaus now com-
mands—Nicklaus said, "Jones is the greatest golfer
who ever lived and probably ever will live. That's my
goal: Bobby Jones. It's the only goal." The same year,
Nicklaus also said, "Ben Hogan is the greatest hitter
of the ball that ever played the game. But I should hit
the ball as well as Hogan someday. Maybe better."

Nicklaus has always been one of Woods's most en-
thusiastic cheerleaders, just as Bobby Jones was one of
Nicklaus's. (Jones's best-known compliment, which
he made after watching Nicklaus, at the age of twenty-
five, win the 1965 Masters, was, "He plays a game with
which I am not familiar." Nicklaus, in a nod to Jones,
made precisely the same remark about Woods after
playing with Woods during the first round of the 2000
PGA Championship, which Woods would go on to
win. Nicklaus, who shot 77 that day, added, "Of
course, I played a game today I wasn't familiar with either.") Woods may be the first player to arise during
Nicklaus's lifetime who is good enough to comprehend the true dimensions of Nicklaus's achievements—just as Nicklaus was probably the first player
who could truly look eye-to-eye at Jones. "I don't know
if anybody can play the way he plays," Nicklaus said in

1999. "He has the ability to do things that nobody else can do." Three years before, after playing a practice round with Woods before the 1996 Masters, when Woods was a twenty-year-old college student and still an amateur, Nicklaus said that Woods could ultimately win the Masters more times than he and Arnold Palmer combined—more than ten times, in other words. "This kid is the most fundamentally sound golfer I've ever seen at almost any age," Nicklaus continued. "I don't know if he's ready to win yet or not. But he will be your favorite for the next twenty years. If he isn't, there's something wrong." Those remarks seemed like hyperbole at the time; now, they don't. (There was nothing spectacular about Woods's showing in Augusta that week; he shot 75-75 and missed the cut, a performance explained in part, perhaps, by the fact that he was in the thick of spring term at Stanford, and had to bring homework with him to Augusta National. But a year later Woods broke Nicklaus's Masters scoring record, and when he won his second Masters, in 2001, he was still younger than Palmer was when Palmer played in his first, in 1955.)

Unlike tennis, golf is not a game of prodigies. Good golf swings are cruelly evanescent, and success on tour depends as much on experience and mental fortitude as on physical skill; the pressures of high-level competition often incapacitate novices, especially during the closing rounds of important tournaments. Even very good players tend to undergo demoralizing apprenticeships. Ben Hogan didn't become the Ben Hogan of myth until he was in his thirties; Tom Watson suffered an early reputation as a choker and didn't win his first tournament until he was nearly twenty-five (by which age Woods had won almost two dozen tour events); David Duval, who is four years older than Woods and briefly supplanted him at the top of the world rankings in 1999, played in eighty-six PGA Tour events as a professional before winning his first. Woods's apprenticeship, in contrast, lasted all of a month: After turning pro in the fall of 1996, he finished third in the fourth tournament he entered, won the next, finished third in the next, and won again the week after that. At the age of twenty-one, he became the youngest player in history (by eight years) to be ranked No. 1 in the world. He has far more career victories than any other active member of the tour, and if his career is of even average duration no player now living has a chance of catching up. In February 2000, he became the tour's leading money winner of all time—a distinction he will surely retain for as long as he plays the game. Sportswriters sometimes define golf's elite as those players who succeed in winning at least one tournament annually for several years in a row. Since turning pro, Woods has averaged one victory every few weeks, despite the fact that he enters fewer events than almost any other of the leading players on tour. In his entire career as a professional he has missed just two cuts (both during weeks when he was ill or exhausted); sportswriters and television commentators now wring their hands and search for hidden causes—swing glitch? overwork? equipment change? romantic setback?—on those rare occasions when he finishes out of a tournament's top ten. He was uncharacteristically winless during the first six tournaments he entered in 2001, prompting some observers to wonder whether he wasn't suffering a slump; he responded by winning five of the next six, including the Masters, the Players Championship, and the Memorial.

o   o   o

STANDING ON THE PRACTICE TEE in Oklahoma, Woods took another question from the grandstands. A young fan asked if he ever felt nervous in golf tournaments. "Oh, my goodness," Woods said, "do I ever get nervous. I get nervous every single time I tee it up in a tournament. That is the honest-to-God truth. And the reason why I say that is because I care. I care about how I play, how I do. Now, if I didn't care, obviously I wouldn't be nervous. But since I'm nervous, that also means I care and I'm trying to do my very best."

He had addressed this same issue earlier in the day, saying, "When I really get nervous is when I have to tee that ball up and hit that first tee shot. Just like anybody, you get a little nervous starting out with your first shot of the day. You may have hit the ball either terrible or great on the driving range, but that's irrelevant. The most important thing is that first shot, and you've got to focus on that shot. What I've found to be the best way to handle pressure is something I took from Harvey Penick, the person who taught Tom Kite and Ben Crenshaw how to play the game. He says you have to make sure that at that moment in time, when you're over that ball, that your shot is the most important thing in your life. That is the kind of focus and dedication you must have to hit a golf shot the way you want to."

No nervousness was evident in Woods's swing that day. He began his exhibition by going through his normal pre-tournament warm-up routine. He said that he likes to arrive at a golf course an hour and a half early and spend ten or fifteen minutes putting. Then he moves to the driving range and hits some shots with his sand wedge, "to get the butterflies out." He said that Nicklaus's warm-up routine had always been to hit pitching wedge, then eight-iron, then four-iron, then three-wood, and then driver, and that he had adopted the same routine except that he substituted sand wedge for pitching wedge. "And then I like to go back to my eight-iron," he said, explaining that he did that in order to reestablish the proper rhythm for his swing. Then, he said, as his tee time approached he envisioned the shot he would have to hit from the first tee and worked on that until he got it right, so that he would feel less nervous when the time came to hit the real thing.

"Notice how easy these swings are," he said, as he hit more balls with his sand wedge. "Balance is the key to these shots. You never hit a wedge shot full."

His shots clicked like the arm of a metronome. "These are your scoring irons. This is where you want to have control and precision."

There was some fidgeting in the grandstands at this point. Some of the spectators had been sitting in the hot sun for a couple of hours or more, and perfectly modulated, feather-soft wedge shots were not what they had been waiting to watch. Woods must have sensed their impatience, because he said, "Now I'm going to try to land this ball on the cart path at the hundred-yard sign." The cart path crossed the range diagonally. He took one shot to get a feel for the distance, then nailed the path with his second. The ball bounced high off the concrete and disappeared down the range. The crowd cheered.

A fierce wind was blowing from right to left across the range, perpendicular to the line of Woods's shots. When he hit a draw—a shot that begins to the right of the target line and bends back to the left—the wind caught the ball and made it curve even more. "That's a lot of hook, isn't it?" he asked. "That just means I have to start the ball a little more at the gallery." There were gasps. He aimed at the far corner of the grandstand to his right and hit a soaring shot that vanished momentarily against the sky before returning to earth in the middle of the range. There were cheers. Then he took a four-iron and hit a shot that had just enough fade—left-to-right curve—to hold it dead straight against the wind.

Controlling a ball in the wind is one of the enduring challenges of golf. The dimples pressed into the surface of a golf ball make it a briskly aerodynamic object—a spherical wing. (If golf balls were smooth, golfers wouldn't be able to bend their shots, and they would have trouble hitting their drives more than a few yards above the ground—as I proved to myself at the driving range one day with an old ball whose skin had been worn nearly featureless. Golf balls without dimples wouldn't fly, just as stitch-less baseballs wouldn't curve.) Good golfers learn how to take advantage of a golf ball's aerial instability by applying English in ways that cause the ball to bend, turn, soar, skid, and perform other useful tricks. Amateur players tend to be most impressed by the ability of the pros to make their balls back up after landing— an effect caused by backspin imparted when a fast-moving clubface makes crisp contact with a ball. But spin has other effects as well, and moving air accentuates or interferes with all of them (as it also does with the flight paths of airplanes); the best golfers learn how to capitalize. Dexterous players who are able to gauge the strength and direction of the wind can often turn it to their advantage. Woods has enough control over his swing to make a shot curve precisely enough in one direction to cancel out a gale blowing in the other.

Woods may have the most extensive arsenal of useful shots in golf, and he is always working on new tricks, often with a particular tournament in mind. Before the 2001 Masters, he spent weeks perfecting a particular soaring three-wood draw, which he had designed specifically for his tee shot on the thirteenth hole at Augusta National. He executed that shot brilliantly during the tournament, and played the thirteenth hole in a cumulative score of three strokes under par over the course of the tournament's four rounds. In Oklahoma, he demonstrated a shot that he had been working on for more than a year, primarily for use in the British Open, which is always held on a seaside course where high winds are common. "It's a new shot for me," he explained, "but it's not a new shot in golf." The shot, he said, had been invented by the great Ben Hogan, whom Woods (like Nicklaus before him) described as "probably the best ball striker who ever lived." Hogan, in turn, had taught it to Claude Harmon, who won the Masters in 1948, and Harmon taught it to his son Butch, who has been Woods's teacher since Woods was seventeen. "So it's one of those things that's not a new shot in the history of golf," he continued, "but it's just a new shot for most players nowadays, because, obviously, they are not privy to that knowledge of the past."

The shot he demonstrated was a low, arrow-straight three-wood shot—which he produced by hitting down on the ball with his club rather than sweeping it off the ground, the conventional technique with fairway woods. In fact, Woods hit down on the ball so crisply that he actually took a substantial divot, something good players almost never do on purpose with their woods. Hitting down on the ball sharply limited its backspin and side spin, causing it to fly straight and low. Reducing the ball's spin reduced its lift, enabling it to cut through the wind without flaring upward and stalling, or veering off to the side. (All golfers quickly learn that low balls travel farther into the wind, but most golfers erroneously assume that the extra distance is caused by "keeping the ball out of the wind"—an impossibility, since the wind blows at ground level, too. Low balls travel farther into the wind because they are spinning less—that's what keeps them low—and balls that spin less are less vulnerable to moving air.)

"Now, how do you hit the low shot—and why would you hit it?" he asked. "Well, why I would hit it is because, one, I'm going to be nervous out there. The longer the ball is in the air, the more time it has to go off line—simple fact. Now, when I'm nervous out there, my ball flight comes down, because I'm trying to keep the ball down on the ground and run it, so it can't get into too much trouble. Another reason is that we play in a lot of wind. People here in Oklahoma understand that. Keeping the ball down is going to help your game, help you shoot lower scores." He teed up a ball. "So I learned this shot last year at the British Open, at Carnoustie, but I didn't have the guts to put it in play. Butch shows it to me that day on the range, in our practice rounds, and I'm hitting it great." Thwack. "Get on the golf course—no chance, not putting it in play yet. I go home and practice it, get it in my repertoire of shots, and now I can hit it pretty good." Thwack. "What I do is I put the ball back in my stance, toward my right heel. Hands ahead. Then, this is the tricky part: go ahead and hit down on it. That's the key—to have the trust to go ahead and take a divot—to punch this three-wood down, take a divot, and drive right through this ball, nice and low." Thwack.

Now Woods pulled out his driver, the club for which he is best known. Woods doesn't lead the tour in driving distance—John Daly has held that title for years—and, in fact, he is often out of the top ten. But few doubt that he could be No. 1 if he wanted to be. (At a press conference before the 1997 Masters, Arnold Palmer said that he had asked another young touring pro how far he thought Woods could hit the ball if he swung all out, and that the young touring pro had said, "Just as far as he wants to.") The tour's driving statistics are based on just two measured drives per tournament round, and Woods doesn't always hit his driver on those holes. If he hit every tee shot as hard as he is capable of hitting it, there is no one in the world who could keep up with him.

"My average drive on tour, I think, is somewhere around 292," he said. "Now, there are times, obviously, when I can hit it a little farther than that, and get a little more out of it. But what I've found is that the harder I hit the ball, the less accuracy I have. The only times I really hit it hard are when I have big fairways, or par-fives that I can possibly reach in two shots, or on holes where it might be an advantage in lengthening one out there and getting over a bunker or getting close enough to go for it."

The PGA Tour's number crunchers place Woods near the middle of the tour ranking in driving accuracy, but that statistic—which is based on the percentage of fairways hit—doesn't reflect what Woods actually does with his tee shots. If, let's say, a pin placement on a particular green is best approached from the farthest left quarter of the fairway, Woods will typically play for that spot (aiming, for all we can tell, at a particular blade of grass). There are many times, in other words, where the middle of the fairway is not his target. If he misses his tee shot by five yards on the left he may end up hitting his approach from the second cut or from the rough, but he has still positioned himself very close to what he believed to be the ideal landing zone. If you have watched him play over an extended period of time—and by this point anyone who consumes a significant amount of televised golf has watched Woods play over an extended period of time—you surely have been struck again and again by his remarkable ability to set himself up for the shot to come. Despite what the tour's statistics sometimes seem to say, no one in golf today exerts as much meaningful control over a driver as Woods does.

He now hit a couple of standard, off-the-shelf drives. They were impressive shots, of course, but his swing was so balanced and seemingly effortless that the crowd remained subdued—he didn't look like he was trying. A young fan shouted something that I couldn't quite hear.

"Over the fence, huh?" Woods said. "What fence are you talking about?" We all turned our eyes to the hazy horizon, perhaps three hundred yards away.

"Oh, my goodness," Woods said.

But he obliged. He aimed for the outside world and launched another drive. I couldn't see far enough to follow the ball all the way back to earth, but I assume it cleared the fence. Even so, Woods hadn't really swung very hard.

"Now, all these drives I've hit so far are about seventy-five or eighty percent of my power," he said.

"The problem with stepping on one, and cranking up the juice a little bit, is that it's hard to keep the ball accurate. I can crank it up, if I need to, to ninety percent, but that's as far as I'll go, because once I go beyond that threshold I start losing my accuracy pretty quickly. So, now I'll crank one up to ninety percent, and you will notice immediately the difference in the speed of the ball as it comes off this club."

He teed up another ball, widened his stance a little bit, and really ripped one. The ball took off like a missile. There were Oohs and Ahs from the crowd. Woods contentedly followed the flight of his shot. "There you go," he said. He teed up another ball. "Now, I'll crank one a little bit beyond ninety, and you'll notice the speed, but, I promise you, I don't really know where it's going besides forward." He teed up another ball, and unleashed another explosion. The crowd cheered.

"Now, there are times when you're going to have to hit a safety shot," Woods continued. "Every single pro who plays on tour has a shot that they will go to on a seventeenth or eighteenth hole—whenever they need to get the ball in the fairway absolutely, at all costs. Now, the safety shot for most players is a cut." A cut is a fade—a shot that, for a right-handed player, starts left and turns right. "Jack Nicklaus, the greatest player of all time, used to hit the ball off the heel on purpose, because he knew that shot would be a low fade every time. I'm not quite that good. He hit the ball off the heel because he knew that if he did the shot was going to be a fade every time, a low fade. The ball wouldn't go very far, that wasn't important. What was important was to get the ball into the fairway. So what I've found is that I like to stand a little bit closer to my golf ball—move in about an inch and a half—and then I try to swing so that the emblem on the back of my glove goes right at the target as long as I possibly can, with more arm speed. The key for me is that I feel my arms are swinging down faster."

The attention of his audience was drifting again; Woods's low fade may be the only shot he hits that even vaguely resembles the shots that most of his fans usually hit: the dreaded screaming banana. (Of course, the average player's screaming banana is nowhere near as straight as Woods's, and it doesn't travel three hundred yards.) Woods turned to a different topic.

"Now I'll hit one like my dad used to, when he used

to try and keep up with me, once he started getting older," he said. He teed up another ball, took a loopy swing, and brought the head of the club down almost directly on top of the ball, which squirted off the front edge of the practice tee. The crowd laughed and applauded—and his father, Earl, who was sitting in a golf cart in front of the grandstand, looked on with no discernible change in his expression.

"I love giving him grief," Woods said. "It's so much fun. Especially when he doesn't have the mike."

Woods then demonstrated what he said was one of his favorite drills, taking four or five different clubs and using each one to hit balls to the same target. "It's a great way to learn speed control of your body and of your arms, and to learn control of the golf ball, because when the wind blows like this you're not going to be hitting the ball very hard. You're going to be trying to keep the ball down." He hit a full nine-iron to the 150-yard marker, then an eight-iron, then a seven, then a six, then a five. With each club, he made the ball land soft enough to "stop on the green"—although there was no actual green for the balls to stop on.

"This is a wonderful way for everyone here who

plays golf to get a better understanding of your game," he said. "It's all predicated on understanding how hard you need to hit the ball for it to go that distance. It's a wonderful way to learn about your game and keep your practices interesting, because, quite frankly, I can't stand out here for four or five hours and hit the same shot every time. It's going to get boring."

Well, this was getting a little boring, too, and the crowd was now truly restless. What almost all the spectators in the stands really wanted to see was a trick they had watched Woods perform in a hugely popular Nike television commercial: bouncing a golf ball on the face of his wedge while passing the club from hand to hand and between his legs and behind his back, and then hitting the ball right out of the air as easily as if it were teed up on the ground. That commercial arose by accident when Woods, feeling bored between takes on a shoot for another Nike commercial, began amusing himself with this stunt, one he had taught himself as a kid. The director, entranced, asked him if he could do that again, and he did so on cue and nearly flawlessly.

Woods now explained how he had taught himself

the trick. "I first learned how to play golf on a par-three golf course," he said. "And on a par-three golf course there are a lot of people out there, and it's always slow. There can be two or three groups on every tee, so there's always about a ten- or fifteen-minute wait on every shot. I was absolutely bored. To kill the time, some of the guys and I started playing with hacky sacks, kicking them around, and then we started bouncing balls on our golf clubs. Next thing you know, we started doing tricks and playing catch and running on the tee boxes and just having a whole bunch of fun playing catch. From there, I've learned how to do it left-handed, and I've learned a few more tricks, too. Just out of pure boredom."

Now the time had come for him to demonstrate. "I heard a rumor that this thing I did on TV was all computerized," he said as he began bouncing the ball on the face of his wedge. "It's kind of a vicious rumor." He passed the club between his legs. "Now, I don't know where that rumor started, whether it was the public or the press, but they obviously hadn't seen me do this before." He bounced the ball up high. "And catch it like this." He stopped the ball, frozen, on the face of his club, let it sit there a moment, then began bouncing it again. "Or I can start out doing it left-handed, if you want me to." Bounce, bounce, bounce. "Or go back to the right." He bounced the ball up over his shoulder from behind, and caught it on the clubface in front. "Now, I didn't put this one in the commercial, because it's the hardest one—it's when you hit the ball off the butt end of the club." He bounced the ball high again, twirled the club so that its shaft was perpendicular to the ground, bounced the ball straight up off the top of the rubber grip, twirled the club back to its former position, and resumed bouncing the ball on the face. "Let's see—it took me four takes to do the Nike spot. Let's see if I can do this out here." He bounced the ball high, took his regular grip on the club, planted his feet, and, just before the ball had fallen all the way back to earth, smacked it more than a third of the way down the range.

°　　　°　　　°

EARLIER IN THE DAY, Woods had worked one-on-one with twenty-five young local golfers, most of whom were members of ethnic minorities. One of the kids had a striped orange-and-black tiger headcover on his driver; another had rolled up the left sleeve of his golf shirt, as Woods sometimes does to keep the sleeve from binding and interfering with the motion of his left arm during his swing. A large number of the golfers used an interlocking grip, in which (on a right-handed golfer) the pinkie of the right hand hooks under the index finger of the left. The interlocking grip is fairly rare in golf—the so-called overlapping, or Vardon, grip is far more popular—but Woods interlocks, and so does Jack Nicklaus. (So, for that matter, does John Daly.) And so did many of the kids.

The clinic's participants, who had been divided into two groups, hit practice balls and looked nervous as Woods worked his way down the line, spending five minutes or so with each child. The quality of the kids' golf swings often deteriorated as he drew near: their nervousness caused them to hurry their tempo, or shorten their backswings, or forget about following through. One panicked-looking youngster, as Woods approached, suddenly seemed unable to make more than glancing contact with a ball. But most of the kids relaxed after Woods had actually stepped up, shaken hands, introduced himself, and said hello. He was friendly and attentive, and he watched the children swing, teed up balls for them, adjusted the positions of their hands or feet, asked questions, made them laugh. "Good swing," he'd say. "Nice shot!" By the time he moved on, almost all of them were smiling. (And—frustrating for the kids—some of them hit their best shots of the day as soon as he had turned his back.) They were also enjoying a small taste of life the way Woods lives it: on the inside of the ropes, with spectators and reporters corralled on the outside.

One of the young golfers was Treas Nelson, a high school junior from Lawton, Oklahoma, who had just won the Class 5A Girls' State Championship by shooting a pair of 73s—a thirty-stroke improvement over her performance in the same tournament the year before. Nelson is the first black golfer in Oklahoma to win a statewide high school title. After she finished her session with Woods, I violated the ban on over-the-rope media fraternization—a ban that was enforced not only by various roving public relations personnel but also by Woods's cadre of Schwarzeneggeresque bodyguards, who were dressed identically in red golf shirts, black golf pants, and two-way-radio headsets, one of whom accompanied

Woods even when he went to the bathroom—and asked her what Woods had told her.

"He said I have the pizza man syndrome," she said. "I get my right hand too much like this." She lifted her right arm with her elbow bent, as though she were holding a pizza on a tray at shoulder height. "He said he has the same problem." She was beaming. Like almost all the kids who received individual instruction, she was wearing Nike shorts and a Nike shirt—goodies provided by Woods's biggest commercial sponsor. (The bodyguards had been dressed by Nike, too.) She had supplemented this uniform with a pair of Nike earrings. "I don't know if he noticed that," she said. But she hoped he had.

Later, I caught up again with Nelson and with another young golfer, Laura Benedix, in an area where talking to them was not forbidden. Benedix, who is white, had won Oklahoma's Class 4A championship. She and Nelson hadn't known each other before, but now they were friends. Since I had seen them last, they had both managed to get the bills of their visors autographed by Woods. I asked Benedix how her lesson had gone.

"It was a blast," she said. "I was taking a long backswing, so he shortened that. And then I like to slide when I come through the ball, instead of turn, so he helped me turn. And I like to pull it, so he was trying to get me to release it more."

I asked them if they had been nervous.

"It wasn't as bad as I thought it would be," Benedix said. "I was trying to stay as calm as I could so that when it was my turn I wouldn't be topping the ball and he would tell me stupid stuff that I already knew."

"He's really nice and relaxed, too," Nelson said. "That's why I wasn't nervous."

A little later, Woods said, "I can relate to these kids. I'm not too far from their age. If these kids saw Jack Nicklaus, I don't think they would have an appreciation for what he's done in the game or what he has to offer, just because of the fact that it's hard for a person of Nicklaus's age to relate to a kid. But I'm not too far removed from my teens. I can say 'Dude,' and that's cool—that's fine."

It's only because of Woods that most of these kids even know who Jack Nicklaus is. Woods spends almost as much time studying golf's history as he does making it, and he goes out of his way to put the game in a long-term context for the youngsters who idolize him.

"When I was young, I looked up to a lot of different players for a lot of different reasons," he said. "Obviously, Jack Nicklaus, who was the greatest of all time. Ben Hogan was the greatest driver there ever was. Seve Ballesteros probably had the best short game. Ben Crenshaw putted the best. So what I did was analyze every different player's game and tried to pick the best out of each and every player and try to look up to that. I wasn't going to look up to just one person."

o   o   o

WHEN THE ONE-ON-ONE instruction sessions were over, Woods took sanctuary in an open tent not far from the driving range. The tent's perimeter had been cordoned off—it was being kept under close surveillance by Woods's bodyguards, whose sunglasses slowly swept back and forth across the crowd, like searchlights on a prison wall—but interested onlookers could lean against the ropes and gape in wonder as Woods drank a Sprite, ate a strawberry, blew his nose, and chatted animatedly with his father. Woods is still impossibly youthful, but he looks much less like a little kid than he did just a couple of years ago; his hairline is ebbing steadily, his face has lost its adolescent angularity, and when he bends or turns you can see that his billowy golf clothes conceal what has gradually become an extraordinary physique. (Woods's musculature, which he has acquired by means of a rigorous but undisclosed weight-lifting program, is most obvious when he is wearing a coat and tie: a sport jacket hangs oddly from his shoulders, as if it weren't quite able to find a comfortable way to drape itself across the muscles in his back. He must be a tailor's nightmare.) He doesn't look overpowering—he's just an inch over six feet tall, and he weighs a good bit less than two hundred pounds—but there doesn't seem to be an ounce of flesh on his body that hasn't been groomed for golf. Nicklaus at the equivalent point in his career was as pudgy as Lumpy Rutherford. (Among Nicklaus's nicknames in his late teens and early twenties were Blob-O and Whaleman; Arnold Palmer and Barbara Nicklaus both called him Fat Boy.)

After Woods composed himself again, he and his father and various representatives of the Tiger Woods Foundation conducted a question-and-answer session in front of the tent. His father spoke first. "I happen to believe that the most important institution in the world is the family and the by-products of that family are the children. . . . The most important thing that any adult will ever have in their entire life is their child. . . . They have been systematically brainwashed so that they can't dream anymore, and if you don't dream you don't have any hope. . . . Golf is a game in which you learn about life." These are familiar themes from Earl, who views his son as proof that thoughtful parenting is worth the trouble.

Few people in the audience were eager to hear from Earl when Tiger was so close at hand. As soon as the father had said his piece, someone asked the son a question. The question had to do with golf's generally lowly public reputation, especially among nonplayers.

"Well, that's changing," he said. "Look how many athletes are picking up the game. You've got one of the biggest sports celebrities of all time, Michael Jordan, playing golf, and he absolutely loves it and wants to be a professional. You have a lot of different athletes from all different sports starting to play it now. Just imagine what it would be like if they had taken up the game at an early age, and golf was their main sport."

This is an intriguing subject for idle sports fan speculation. There has never been a great golfer who couldn't in some sense be considered a great athlete, especially in the category of eye-hand coordination; but conventional wisdom has usually held that golfers don't need the sort of raw physical aptitude that other athletes do, and that golf is as much a mental game as it is a physical one. (It would be hard to picture Craig Stadler, for example, setting a world record in the long jump or even chasing down a line drive deep in center field. But Stadler—whose nickname, Walrus, refers both to his drooping mustache and his lumbering girth—did win the Masters, in 1982.) In recent years, though, professional golfers have begun to pay much more attention to physical conditioning. They don't smoke nearly as many cigarettes as Hogan and Palmer used to, for example, and they don't drink anything like as much liquor as touring pros once routinely did, and they spend a lot more time not only on the driving range but also in the gym. Much of the recent gain in driving distance on tour is surely a reflection of the pros' newfound respect for robust health. The example of Woods's disciplined training is partly responsible for that, but his biggest impact may not be seen for years. By making golf seem not only extraordinarily exciting (and phenomenally remunerative) but also athletically respectable, Woods has increased the likelihood that the current crop of athletically gifted grade school athletes might take up golf as their principal sport rather than using the game merely to unwind between soccer or basketball seasons. Woods's allure is so strong that the tour twenty years from now could conceivably be filled with players who look and live and think like real athletes.

This is not to say that mere athleticism is necessarily an overwhelming advantage in golf. Michael Jordan and Ivan Lendl, two of the most monumentally gifted athletes of their generation, have had far less success as golfers than either expected when he took up the game, despite having made considerable expenditures of effort, time, and money in the hope of becoming good players. A nongolfer might think that a couple of athletic superstars like those two would be able to conquer a game like golf in a snap, but both men, while becoming adept country-club-level players, have nonetheless failed by far to live up to their own dreams. Lendl is officially a pro—he has competed in the Czech Open and a handful of ultra-low-level professional events—but there is next to no chance that you will ever see his name in the field at any of golf's Grand Slam events. (Lendl belongs to a nine-hole golf club that plays an annual two-day match with a nine-hole golf club that I belong to, and he is regularly beaten by a good golf buddy of mine, our club champion, who installs septic tanks for a living.) But athletic ability is not irrelevant in golf, and Woods has changed the way athletes think of the game. As he himself put it, a physically talented boy or girl is now far more likely to look beyond "your typical core sports in America" when dreaming of future athletic glory. That's brand new, and it's all because of Woods.

A young fan asked Woods if he had a favorite golf course.

"I really don't, to be honest with you," he said. "But I have a style that I love: I love links golf courses."

"Links," contrary to what many people believe, is not a synonym for "golf course"; it is a term for a particular type of terrain, found mainly in the British Isles—sandy seaside dune land, which was deeply submerged under ice and ocean during the Ice Age,

and rose above sea level when the huge ice cap re-
treated. The world's first golf courses were built on
links land, which was available for recreation because
it was so wind-wracked and desolate that it was of no
conceivable commercial interest to anyone but
sheep farmers, whose flocks were the world's first
greens mowers. All modern golf courses can trace
their genetic heritage to British links courses—and
especially to the great granddaddy of them all, the
Old Course at St. Andrews, in Scotland. The shel-
tered valleys between grassy dunes became the first
fairways; the first bunkers were just shallow sandy pits
worn into the sides of dunes by sheep huddling to
protect themselves from the wind. To love links
courses is to love the ancient history of the game—a
mark of good taste in a golfer. Woods's love for links
courses is also emblematic of his appetite for new
challenges.

"We don't get to play links courses here in the
States," he continued. "There are only a few—only a
handful. But over in Scotland and Ireland and England, those are the true links golf courses of the
world, where wind like this"—the gusts in Oklahoma
City that day were measured at forty miles an hour—

"is considered a calm day, and it's usually raining and it's cold, and you're playing out in the elements, and everything changes from day to day. This year, the British Open is going to St. Andrews. I played in the Dunhill Cup there. The first hole is something like a three-hundred-and-seventy-yard par-four. One day, I hit three-iron from the tee, then sixty-degree sand wedge to the green, and the very next day, I hit a driver and a four-iron—the same hole—just because the wind and elements had changed."

Earl spoke up and told a story about Tiger, at the age of seventeen, playing in the British Open with Greg Norman.

"Nineteen," Tiger corrected. "You're having a senior moment again."

The crowd laughed, and Earl got about three quarters of the way to a smile. The onstage byplay between Earl and Tiger doesn't quite amount to a standup routine, but they pick on each other in a good-humored way. They seem to do it partly for comedic effect and partly out of their own profoundly competitive natures. The night before, at the fund-raising dinner, Earl had told a slightly rambling story about a match that Tiger had played when he was very young. Tiger had been paired with an older boy who was taller and heavier than he was, and who drove the green on the first hole of their match. When that match was over, Tiger confessed to his father than he had been afraid while he was playing, because his opponent had seemed so big and strong. "Did you beat him?" Earl asked. Tiger acknowledged that he had, and at that moment Tiger realized that he didn't need to be afraid of bigger or stronger kids—a useful lesson, Earl said, for a ten-year-old world beater. "Eleven!" Tiger shouted from his table, correcting his father's estimate of his age at the time. (When Tiger took the podium himself, a little later, he said that Earl provided proof of his belief in the importance of dreaming big dreams: "He thinks he's better than I am.")

Here in front of the tent, Tiger fielded a question from a very young fan, who wanted to know how old he had been when he started playing.

"I believe it was eleven months," Tiger said, and he looked to Earl for confirmation.

"You've been correcting me so far," Earl said. "Correct yourself."

2 CREATING TIGER WOODS

A FEW HOURS before Woods's Oklahoma City exhibition, I sat with the all-black congregation of the St. John Missionary Baptist Church (Motto: "We Strive to Be 'The Best Church This Side of Judgement' ") while Tiger's father gave a guest sermon. Earl's talk was preceded by hymns, prayers, and half a dozen full-immersion baptisms, which were conducted in a large tank that was visible through an opening in the wall above the altar. His subject was his only subject. "Tiger was not created to be a golfer," he said. "Tiger was made to be a good person, and that was first and foremost in our family."

Earl is shorter and considerably wider than Tiger, and he is a walking anthology of alarming health problems. He is a heavy and largely unapologetic cigarette smoker; it's a habit he picked up in the Army, and one that his son finds disgusting and has pushed his father to shake. ("I know smoking is wrong," Earl himself once told Rick Reilly of *Sports Illustrated,* "but I contend there's no cholesterol in a cigarette.") He suffers from advanced heart disease. He underwent quadruple bypass surgery in the 1980s and was hospitalized with coronary problems again in October 1996 while Tiger was competing in the Tour Championship at Southern Hills Country Club, in Tulsa, Oklahoma. Concern about his father's condition distracted Tiger during that tournament and contributed to his shooting his worst score ever as a member of the PGA Tour: 78 in the second round. Four months later, Earl underwent triple bypass surgery, then had surgery again after ripping out the grafts with hiccups. Earl has also undergone radiation treatment for prostate cancer and has endured a variety of lesser medical emergencies. His brushes with death have not inspired him to transform his lifestyle, however, and he often appears to be struggling when moving under his own power; he has to catch his breath after almost any significant physical exertion.

He has a good speaking voice, though—a preacher's voice. It caught in his throat a couple of times during his sermon, despite the fact that he has given essentially the same presentation dozens if not hundreds of times before. "Sometimes when I talk about my son I get very emotional," he explained. "So bear with me." He often rambles in puzzling directions when speaking extemporaneously—I once heard him refer to Tiger as "brain-damaged," a jarring remark that he made in passing and didn't explain—but he was in good form that morning in church.

Earl Woods was born in Manhattan, Kansas, during the Great Depression. He had an older brother and four older sisters. His mother had earned a college degree, but because she was black she could find work only as a housemaid. His father was a brick mason and a gardener and a frustrated athlete, and he dreamed of a baseball career for his son. (The father's closest personal contact with baseball in adulthood was as a scoreboard operator at a local park where only white teams were allowed to play.) The family was poor—Earl remembers receiving charity food baskets from the local Rotary Club at

Thanksgiving—but the Woods children did not feel impoverished. His mother was loving and protective, and she was evangelical on the subject of education. She forbade Earl to stay home from school during snowstorms, asked his teacher to increase his workload when he showed signs of slacking off, and admonished him, in connection with one of his early athletic heroes, "Don't you dare talk the way Joe Louis talks when you grow up!" Earl, in turn, passed versions of these lessons along to Tiger, who had a distinguished record at every stage in his education and, unlike most other students with athletic scholarships, took a full load of regular academic courses when he was in college, at Stanford.

Earl's secure world came apart when he was eleven: his father died suddenly of a stroke, and his mother died two years later, at least partly of grief. (Earl recalls the pain of watching her ceaselessly rocking in a rocking chair while humming the hymn "What Are They Doing in Heaven Today?") He was raised from that point by his eldest sister, who had absorbed her mother's powerful example and who succeeded in keeping the children together in the home in which they had grown up. Earl attended a mostly white high school and played catcher on an otherwise all-white American Legion baseball team. He endured numerous racist taunts when he was on the ball field—as did the other members of his family, who were often the only black fans in the grandstands. In high school he was a popular candidate for "king of the prom," but he says that the election was rigged against him by adults who did not want to see a black king kiss a white queen. He got through it all with the support of his siblings and with the help of a powerful sense of self-worth, which he attributes to his mother. She had taught him—as he would later teach Tiger—that racism is evidence of a defect in the racist, not in the racist's victim. He needed to apply the same lesson when he attended his hometown college, Kansas State University, on an athletic scholarship, and became the first black baseball player in the conference known today as the Big Twelve. He lived at home and commuted by bicycle.

After graduation, Earl briefly played semiprofessional baseball, then reluctantly turned down a chance to play in the Negro Leagues—a job that would have fulfilled his father's dream for him—and spent twenty years in the Army, where he felt he would have a bigger and better future. The day before he entered the service, he married Barbara Hart; they eventually had three children, two sons and a daughter, to whom he was a remote father at best. (Those children, who now have children of their own, are named Earl, Kevin, and Royce.) He served two widely separated tours of duty in Vietnam, the second as a Green Beret, and later taught military history at the City College of New York. It was in Southeast Asia that he met two of the most important figures in his adult life: Vuong Dang "Tiger" Phong, a South Vietnamese lieutenant colonel, who was his colleague, close friend, and protector during the war; and Kultida Punsawad, a Thai office receptionist, who would later become his second wife. After the fall of Saigon in 1975, Earl vowed to himself that if he and Kultida had a son, he would give the boy the nickname of his old friend Colonel Phong, whom he credited with having more than once saved his life.

Earl can be disconcertingly vague about the details of his life. I once asked him in what year he and Kultida had been married, and he said, "Hell, I don't know." He then laughed and said he had no memory for that sort of thing, and that I should ask his wife instead. (They were married in 1969; they had met three years before.) Tom Callahan, a columnist and regular contributor to *Golf Digest,* says that when he first met Earl, in 1996, he didn't believe that Earl had actually been in the military. "I asked him when he had been in Vietnam, and he couldn't tell me," Callahan, a former Marine, said. "Now, I can tell you the day I got to Quantico and the hour I left—but Earl can't tell me when he was in Vietnam? So I asked him just to give me a general idea—for example, was he there before Tet? He said, 'When was Tet?' Here's a career Army officer, and yet he can't tell me when the Tet Offensive was—come on. So I ended up requesting his military records through the Freedom of Information Act, and what I thought I would find out was that he hadn't been in the service at all. But, of course, it came back that he had been in twice, just as he said, and that he really had been in the Green Berets. I guess that's just the way his mind works."

In 1997, on assignment from *Golf Digest,* Callahan set out to track down Tiger Phong. Earl had said many times that he hoped word of his son's achievements as a golfer would someday reach Phong—with whom he had had no contact since the American withdrawal—and that Phong would realize that the best golfer in the world had been named in his honor. Callahan's quest was complicated by the fact that Earl, characteristically, had misremembered his old friend's name as Nguyen, rather than Vuong. But Callahan persevered, and even traveled to Vietnam; through sheer journalistic tenacity, and at occasional risk to his own safety, he eventually learned that Phong had died in 1976, at the age of forty-seven, in a Communist labor camp. (Callahan eventually saw Phong's bones, which his family had preserved, and a photograph of them ran in the magazine.) He also learned that Phong's widow had lived in Tacoma, Washington, since 1994 and had never heard of Tiger Woods. Callahan's discovery led to a emotional meeting between the two families, at which Tiger for the first time met relatives of the man his father had always called "Tiger One."

Earl retired from the Army in 1974, with the rank of lieutenant colonel, and he and Kultida moved out of New York, where Earl had been teaching, and settled in California. Eldrick Tiger Woods was born on December 30, 1975. His parents selected his first name because it began and ended with the initials of their own names, an orthographic reminder to themselves of their total commitment to this child.

Earl was determined to be a better parent to the last of his four children than he had been to the first three, and his retirement from the Army gave him more time to be attentive. His one significant distraction—other than his job, as a contract administrator and materials manager at McDonnell Douglas, in Huntington Beach, California—was golf, a game at which he had become remarkably proficient despite having taken it up little more than a year earlier, at the age of forty-two. (Playing mostly on a scrappy military golf course near their home, he quickly reduced his handicap to zero—a rate of progress almost unheard of in golf, whose players often require a decade or more of hard work to become even mediocre.) He tuned his swing in the evenings by hitting balls into a net in his garage, and he often placed his infant son in a high chair beside him, so the two of them could commune while he practiced. "It was a way of spending time together," he said—a typical golfer's rationalization, although in this case it appears the baby was a more than willing spectator. Far from being bored, Tiger was captivated by the motion. One momentous day, when he was still young enough not to have mastered all the finer points of walking, he astonished his father by climbing down from his high chair, picking up a baby-sized plastic club, and executing a passable imitation of Earl's quite good golf swing. Tiger made that first swing left-handed—a mirror image of his right-handed model. A few days later, he stepped around the ball, correctly reversed his grip, and made an equally precocious swing from the opposite side. At that moment, Earl realized he was the steward of an extraordinary talent.

Signs that the new child was special had been evident from before the beginning, according to Earl. "When Tida was seven months pregnant with Tiger," he has written, "I was invited to play in a golf tournament at Lake Shastina in northern California. We drove there, and Tida walked the golf course with me." The baby squirmed and kicked, except when the Woodses drew close to any putting green. "Then, whenever a golf ball hit the green, it reverberated against the volcanic surface and produced a thumping sound, similar to a drum. Tiger apparently reacted to these vibrations. He would suddenly be very still and quiet"—as well-behaved spectators always are when golfers are preparing to putt. Earl's conclusion: "He seemed to know golf protocol while he was still in the womb."

As the years went by, this incident and others led Earl to believe that the birth of his son had been—as he told the St. John congregation—"the plan of the man upstairs." Looking back on his life, he detected a pattern of trials and tests and close escapes from tragedy, and he decided that God had been grooming him all along for something big. He remembered a day in Vietnam when his life had been spared twice: first, when a sniper's bullets narrowly missed him; and later, when his friend Tiger Phong warned him about a poisonous snake lurking inches from his head. He came to view his first marriage as a sort of providential dry run for his second, and to think of his first two sons almost as rough drafts for his third. (In Earl's autobiography, the chapter concerning this period is called "Marriages and Mulligans.") He blamed himself for not taking an active role in the upbringing of his first three children, but he also decided that his negligence had been a necessary phase in his preparation for what he now believed to be the true purpose of his life: the creation and nurturing of Tiger Woods. He hadn't been a good father, he realized, but without those early failures he would never have learned how to become a better father now.

As young Eldrick grew, Earl was struck more and more by what he described in church that day as "the charismatic power that resides in my son Tiger"—a power that he had otherwise noticed only in Nelson Mandela, Mahatma Gandhi, and a handful of other figures. (Tiger has met Mandela, an encounter that Earl described this year in a quote in *TV Guide:* "It was the first time Tiger met a human being who was equal to him, who was as powerful as Tiger is. He told Tiger he had a lot to give the world. He saw himself in Tiger.") Golf, Earl began to believe, was not the true purpose of Tiger's life, but was merely one of the instruments by which he would one day influence the course of civilization. The boy's talents were too astonishing not to have some deeper purpose; how else could his father make sense of this remarkable prodigy? Earl saw manifestations of divine influence in Tiger's competitive record, his golf swing, his work ethic, his ease in front of television cameras, and in

Earl's own ability at critical moments to transmit encouragement and advice to his son by means of mental telepathy. (Earl says that he communicated telepathically with Tiger—and urged him to trust his putting stroke—at a crucial moment during the 1999 PGA Championship, which Earl was watching on TV and which Tiger went on to win.) Earl even came to view his own ill health as a God-given gift; its purpose, he says, was to teach him (so that he, in turn, could teach his son) that life is short: seize the day.

"Tiger has already transcended the game of golf," Earl has said. "He is a world figure, not just a world golf figure. He has transcended athletics already. He is a spokesperson. He is a world celebrity. The next step is to be someone on the world scale who makes an impact on humanity, and that is what he is going to be doing. He is going to make a difference in people's lives all over the world. In what areas? I don't know yet, because it hasn't come. But it's coming."

Even to someone sitting in a church pew, this might sound mystical and wacky—and yet the more you learn about Tiger Woods's preternatural relationship to the game of golf, the easier it becomes to understand why terrestrial interpretations seem inadequate to Earl. Of course, Earl's explanation has the substantial benefit for him of making his early failures as a parent seem to have been divinely ordained: he is, in effect, forgiving himself for not being a better person. But when he speaks or writes in this vein he doesn't seem cynical, or even particularly self-serving. He is as mystified by the scale of his son's achievements as everyone else is, and he is too much in awe of them to take full credit for himself. As he told the congregation, "I'm good, but I'm not that good."

When Tiger was still a toddler, Earl says, the child was able to identify the swing flaws of adult players. ("Look, Daddy," Tiger would say, "that man has a reverse pivot!") Tiger putted with Bob Hope on the *Mike Douglas Show* at the age of two, broke 50 for nine holes at the age of three, hit golf balls on *That's Incredible!* at the age of five, and received his first autograph request when he was still too young to have a signature. (The television performances grew out of a chance appearance on a local news show in California.) He was aware of his gift, and remarkably comfortable with it. In one frequently shown piece of old footage, a smiling and impossibly young-looking Tiger Woods, his golf cap pushed back high on his head, happily says, "I want to win all the big tournaments—the major ones—and I hope to play well when I get older, and beat all the pros." He looks so cute and innocent that his comment would break your heart if you didn't know what he's done since then. Before he had learned to count to ten, Earl says, Tiger could tell you, on any golf hole, where each member of a foursome stood in relation to par. While his grade school contemporaries drew pictures of racing cars and robots, Tiger sketched the trajectories of his irons. He came from behind to win the Junior World Championship, in San Diego, against an international field, when he was eight.

"Something that I think no one really knows," Woods said shortly before his exhibition in Oklahoma, "is that the Junior World was where my confidence started—knowing that I could play this game against a high level of players—and from then on I felt like I could compete against the best players anywhere around the world." He won the same tournament four more times as well, at the ages of nine, twelve, thirteen, and fourteen.

More than anything else, Woods loved to compete. "He gets that from me," Earl says. "We were very competitive when he was a little kid. We had fun through competition. Tiger is the ultimate competitor, always has been, always will be. And we just enjoyed competitive situations. Every practice was a competition. We played games—and it's still that way. When I drive a ball now, Tiger says, 'Is that the best you can do?' And I tell him, 'Well, I can beat your butt on the putting green.' And he says, 'No, you can't—not anymore.' You see, I used to have an advantage, because I was taller, and my lag putting was a lot better than his. Now he's taller than I am, and his lag putting is better than mine." As Tiger's skills grew, Earl helped him mentally prepare for competition by putting him through (with Tiger's advance consent) what he called his "Finishing School"—an extended period of psychological hazing on the golf course, which was intended to harden Tiger's nerves for tournament play and gradually inoculate him against a broad spectrum of distractions. When the two played together, Earl would tee up his own ball on the wrong side of the markers, improve his lie, jingle change in his pockets as Tiger was preparing to putt, clap his hands, make rude noises, and do everything he could think of to break his son's concentration. Earl's program helped to hone Tiger's ability to remain focused while competing—one of the most impressive of his many athletic talents, and one that is probably unequaled in sports. Tiger's concentration is so acute that he probably receives less credit for it than he deserves, because he makes it seem easy. No athlete in history has ever competed day in and day out under the burden of such intense public fascination. His appearance remains so serene as the pressure mounts that you tend to forget about the trying conditions under which he performs. Golf fans simply assume that he is going to win, and time and again over the years he has found startling new ways to exceed their expectations. Earl has said that Tiger simply doesn't feel pressure—that he "has no comfort level," as he once told me, meaning that there is no level of competitive intensity at which he falls apart—but it's probably more accurate to say that Tiger has found ways to turn pressure to his own advantage, to harness it, to use it as a fuel. He doesn't respond to pressure the way you and I would, and part of the credit for that has to go to Earl.

One of Earl's most striking attributes as a teacher—and one that distinguishes him from certain other high-profile fathers of great athletes—is his understanding of his own limitations. He realized very early that there was a point beyond which he would be unable to help his son. He did not, for example, insist on being his son's only coach. The most important periods in the evolution of Tiger's swing were supervised not by Earl but, first, by a young teaching pro named Rudy Duran, who taught him at a short, scrappy par-three course called Heartwell, which was situated near the Woods house and was exactly the right size for a talented preschooler who couldn't yet hit a ball a hundred yards, and, later, by Butch Harmon, who has been his coach since he was seventeen. Earl was a good enough player to help out, especially on the putting green, but his most important role was not as a technician but as an indefatigable cheerleader. He built a high floor under his son's self-confidence, repeatedly assuring him that he was special, that he had an otherworldly gift, that he had been chosen for great things. This may be the single most powerful weapon in Tiger's competitive arsenal today: his absolute conviction that he deserves to win every tournament he enters.

On a golf course, Tiger first beat his father, by a single stroke, with a score of 71, when he was eleven. This was a watershed event not only for the son but also for the father, who found that his own competitive desire was suddenly gone, and realized that from now on the thrill of victory for him would be vicarious. That same summer, Tiger entered thirty-three junior tournaments and won them all. ("That's when I peaked," Tiger says. "It's been downhill since.") When he was a freshman in high school, his cumulative tournament score for the year was one under par, a mark that beat the next best varsity player at his school by more than forty strokes. At fifteen, he became the youngest player ever to win the United States Junior Amateur Championship—and then the only player in history to win it three years in a row. At sixteen, he competed in a regular event on the PGA Tour, the Nissan Los Angeles Open. (He missed the cut.) Throughout his teens, he won so many tournaments, first as a high school player and then as a college student, that his trophies and awards began to displace furniture in the Woodses' modest family home.

Woods's first U.S. Amateur victory introduced him to a broad audience of golf fans. That tournament took place at the Tournament Players Club at Sawgrass, in Ponte Vedra Beach, Florida, in 1994. In the final, Woods faced Trip Kuehne, who was a highly talented junior at Oklahoma State University and a friend. (Kuehne's sister, Kelli, won the women's U.S. Amateur in 1995 and 1996 and now plays on the LPGA Tour, where she won the 1999 Corning Classic; his brother, Hank, won the U.S. Amateur in 1998. Tiger and Kelli have competed as teammates in mixed professional events, and they were once linked romantically by various tabloids, though they have never been more than friends.)

The U.S. Amateur is conducted at match play, a form of competition in which each hole is a separate contest that a player either wins, loses, or ties. The outcome of the match is determined not by the total number of strokes taken, as in stroke play, but by the number of holes won. The match ends as soon as either player has built a lead that exceeds the number of holes remaining, and outcomes are described according to a convention that sometimes confuses the uninitiated: a player who is two holes ahead with one hole left to play is said to have won the match "two and one"; a player who is one hole ahead after seventeen holes and then wins the final hole as well is said to have won "two up." In an eighteen-hole match, the most cataclysmic possible victory would be "ten and eight"—meaning that the victor had won each of the first ten holes, leaving the loser with no hope of recovery after playing just one hole on the second nine. A player who leads a match by exactly the number of holes remaining is said to be "dormie"—a word that is presumably derived from the French verb *dormir,* meaning to sleep. (A player who is dormie can snooze the rest of the way in, since the laggard can now hope for no better than a tie.) In the U.S. Amateur, an elimination tournament, ties are played out by continuing the match beyond the stipulated end until one player or the other wins a hole. (If an eighteen-hole match is tied after eighteen holes and continues for two extra holes, the victor is said to have won in "twenty holes.") In the Amateur, preliminary matches are eighteen holes long; the final is thirty-six, with the first eighteen played during the morning on the last day of the tournament and the second eighteen played after lunch.

In the 1994 Amateur final, Kuehne got off to a daunting start, building a six-hole lead over the first thirteen holes. Ordinarily in match play, a lead like Kuehne's is considered insurmountable; in the century-long history of the U.S. Amateur, no player had ever come back to win after being so far behind at any point in a match. Kuehne showed no sign of collapsing; he continued to play steadily, and with just twelve holes left to play in the afternoon round, he still led by five holes. His victory seemed assured, because at that point, all he had to do to secure the title was to win four of the remaining holes, or tie eight of them.

But Woods never lost his focus. Although he was still just a kid, he already had a long history of taking important matches down to the wire. All three of his Junior Amateur titles had been squeakers; one of those matches had lasted eighteen holes, and the other two had lasted nineteen. (In the second of the two that went to extra holes, Woods was two down with two to go and then won three holes in a row. On the seventeenth green, Woods had an eight-foot putt for birdie, which he had to sink in order to keep the match going. He told his caddie, Jay Brunza, who also served as his sports psychologist, "Got to be like Nicklaus. Got to will this in the hole." And he did.*)

---

*Can a golfer really will a ball into the hole? The explanation, I think, is that certain great athletes—among them Nicklaus and Woods—somehow have the ability to maintain an exceptional level of physical composure while under intense mental pressure. Facing a ten- or twenty-foot putt to win a tournament or keep a match alive, they don't suddenly tense up even slightly, or squeeze their putter tighter, or break into a sweat as the rest of us would do in far less trying circumstances. Instead, they stroke the putt exactly as they would have stroked it on the practice green, or maybe even a little better. You can often see the same effect in the final minutes of a closely fought basketball game, when players who have been swishing baskets all night suddenly begin to bounce balls off the rim—a malady that can sometimes infect an entire team. The cause, I believe, is that the pressure level has risen to the point where the players' muscles are not responding quite the way they did earlier in the game. The players' bodies become physically different in their reactions, and the players begin to misfire very slightly, and their shots land wide of the mark. The great players are the ones—like Michael Jordan—who for some reason don't respond to pressure in the same way. Like Nicklaus and Woods, Jordan is able to make the ball do what he wants it to do at moments when everything is at stake.

Those experiences reinforced his already daunting self-confidence. He had come back from the edge of defeat many times before; why not now? At some point that day, Earl—who had traveled with him to Florida—caught up with his son and issued a terse final instruction: "Let the legend grow."

Golf matches are emotionally complex. In stroke play, a player can almost choose a target blood pressure rate and try to maintain it from start to finish; this is what the pros are referring to when they talk about "playing within yourself." Match play is trickier, and more volatile. If my opponent has an easy putt for birdie on some hole, then a par from me would make no more difference to the match than would a triple-bogey, so I have to try to make a birdie, too, even if that means I attempt an absurdly difficult shot that has next to no chance of going in the hole. Similarly, if my opponent can do no better than a bogey, I would be foolish to try a risky shot in the hope of making a birdie, because a nice safe par will win me the hole—as long as I don't turn so conservative that I lose my competitive edge. In match play, golfers often have to adjust their emotions and their styles of play from moment to moment as the conditions of the competition change. At the same time, they have to be careful not to become too conservative when they are leading or too recklessly aggressive when they're behind. In 1995, I watched the thirty-six-hole final match of the Kansas Amateur Championship, which was played in Kansas City. The match was between a terrifically talented younger player and a cagey older veteran. The younger player built a big lead and looked as though he had the match well in hand, but he then throttled back, protecting his lead and trying not to make stupid mistakes. As soon as he did, the older player—who had been close to despair—won a hole. Suddenly, the younger player's big lead didn't seem quite so big to either of them anymore, and the mood of the match was transformed. In the space of a few moments the younger player went from looking as though he owned the world to looking as though he had just stepped off a cliff—even though in reality the only difference was a single swing of the club. Confidence gone, the younger player began losing holes, and the older player was suddenly reanimated. The younger player eventually won, but the match went thirty-six holes and wasn't decided until the very end. For a spectator walking alongside the players, the match was an emotional roller-coaster ride.

The 1994 U.S. Amateur was a roller-coaster ride, too—although one in which the cars seemed to climb the track inexorably almost all day long, then suddenly plunge over the edge. That's how it had to feel for Kuehne, at any rate. Hole after hole, Woods seemed to be going nowhere. He was playing decently, but Kuehne was brilliant, yet Woods never became discouraged, and just at the point when the match had begun to seem out of his reach, he began to erode Kuehne's lead, winning four of the five holes between the seventh and the eleventh. In a relative blink of an eye, the psychology of the match turned inside out. Fans who had thought that Woods didn't have a chance now believed that Kuehne would never win another hole. It must have seemed that way to the competitors as well.

Woods was relentless, and he finally took the lead himself for the first time all day with a birdie at the seventeenth hole, which was the thirty-fifth hole of the match. His shot into that green was one of the most thrilling I've ever seen. (I was watching on TV, in the grill room of my golf club at home.) The seventeenth at Sawgrass may be the most instantly recognizable golf hole in the world: it's a par-three whose green is an island—a treacherously small circle of undulating turf surrounded by a lake, from which the club annually harvests tens of thousands of errant balls. The flag that day was situated on the far right side, just a few paces from the water, and Woods did something that sensible players never do: he aimed directly at it. The shot so unnerved Kultida—who was watching the match on television, at home in California—that she fell to the floor from her bed when he hit it, according to Tim Rosaforte, who covered the match for *Sports Illustrated*. ("That boy tried to kill me," she said later.) Tiger's ball missed the water by just a few feet, leaving him with a fourteen-foot putt for birdie. Which—of course—he made.

∘　　∘　　∘

WHEN WOODS FIRST began to attract national attention, people often assumed that the real motivating force behind his game must be the oldest one in modern sports: a pushy father with frustrated ath-

letic aspirations and a powerful yearning for un-
earned income. In early 1998, the sportswriter John
Feinstein published a short, mean-spirited book
called *The First Coming: Tiger Woods—Master or Mar-
tyr?,* in which he compared Earl to the notoriously
manipulative father of the tennis prodigy Jennifer
Capriati, who burned out on the women's tour at seventeen. (She has since returned, after a harrowing
interval during which, among other things, she was
arrested for possession of marijuana; in 2001, she
won the Australian and French Opens and has
reestablished herself as one of the dominant players
on the women's tour.) "Both fathers willingly turned
their children into meal tickets long before they had
turned pro," Feinstein wrote, and in the years since
the book appeared he has often made similar remarks, commenting on a television special that Earl
"saw in Tiger, very early, someone who could make
him rich and famous."

But Feinstein is clearly wrong. Earl isn't shy about
standing in front of microphones or television cameras, or about celebrating his own contributions to
his son's success. ("You are cursed to have the opportunity to speak to the Earl of Woods," he grandly said

to me once, upon returning a telephone call.) But there is no hint of venality in his conduct. He still lives in the house where Tiger grew up, he still tirelessly answers reporters' questions about his son, and he still plays an active (and, for him, an often exhausting) role in the Tiger Woods Foundation. He hasn't bought himself a jet, he hasn't surrounded himself with actresses, and he hasn't draped himself in gold. Judged solely by the material circumstances of his life, Earl seems less like a Svengali than like an overworked low-level retainer in Tiger's entourage. He doesn't run Tiger's life; he runs his own life as though nothing but Tiger's life mattered.

Far from exploiting his son's celebrity, Earl sometimes seems to be sacrificing his own well-being for what he clearly believes to be a higher cause. One of the services he has performed has been relieving the intense media pressure on his son by making himself available for the kinds of open-ended personal interviews that Tiger no longer gives; Earl stands on the front porch and answers questions while Tiger slips out the back. That contribution isn't utterly selfless on Earl's part, because he likes the limelight, but it's a major contribution nonetheless; Tiger's life would be a lot more hectic and exhausting if Earl weren't around to play decoy.

It has become increasingly clear over the years that Tiger's drive has always been internal, and that while Earl and Kultida may have been its facilitators, they were not its authors. When Tiger was still very young, for example, he memorized his father's office telephone number so he could call Earl each afternoon to ask if the two of them could practice at the golf course after work. Tiger has written that Earl "would always pause for a second or two—keeping me in suspense—but he always said yes." Earl was a tireless and innovative practice companion and coach, but he believed that the initiative must always come from the boy. Wayne Gretzky was once approached by a pushy father who wanted Gretzky to tell his son that if he wanted to get anywhere as a hockey player he had to practice. "Nobody ever told me to practice," Gretzky said. Tiger was the same way.

Far from having pushed their son, the Woodses sometimes worried that his infatuation with golf was eclipsing other parts of his life. "In junior golf, I was all out," Tiger said in Oklahoma. "My parents would say, You can't play, you're playing too much—but I wanted to play every tournament, and play twice in one day." Earl repeatedly urged him, with little success, to try other sports. (He did go out for track and cross-country in high school, and Earl believes—with no confirmation from anyone else—that he could have been a world-class runner, but his involvement didn't last long. "One year I grew four inches," Tiger says, "and there went that idea.") Earl once fretted that Tiger was so focused on winning that he had ceased to enjoy himself on the golf course. Tiger replied curtly, "That's how I enjoy myself, by shooting low scores." After that, Earl kept his opinions to himself.

Kultida used golf as an incentive—for example, by forbidding her son to hit practice balls until he had finished his homework. "My wife was the disciplinarian in the family," Earl says, "and I was the friend. She set the standard that in this house education comes first, you will get your homework done before you practice. And he bought into that, and he still buys into that, and he tells that to the kids. That is one of the best things he ever learned from his mother."

Although Earl and Kultida did not force Tiger to become a golfer, they both made enormous sacrifices to help him realize his dreams. They didn't take a vacation in twenty years, because every spare dollar was needed to transport Tiger to and from tournaments. Earl estimates that the family's annual travel expenses during Tiger's junior golf years amounted to as much as thirty thousand dollars, a sum Earl couldn't have covered without a succession of home equity loans. Kultida was an infinitely patient chauffeur, rising long before dawn to drive Tiger to distant tournaments (and reminding him to bring his pillow so that he could go back to sleep in the car). Most of Earl's free time away from work was consumed by Tiger's insatiable appetite for practice. All these sacrifices were made without complaint. Both parents believed that their son's needs must always come before their own, and they were determined that the only impediment to his success—in golf or in whatever other field he might choose to pursue—would be the level of his own desire.

Earl's and Kultida's sacrifices took a toll on their marriage. They have lived apart for several years now—Earl lives in the old family home, while Kultida lives in a new house that Tiger bought for her—although they have not divorced. Their unorthodox living arrangement inevitably comes to mind when Earl says, as he did in church in Oklahoma on the day he appeared as a guest preacher, "The family is the most important institution in the world." How important can the family be if he no longer seems to be a part of one?

The answer is that Earl doesn't view his own domestic situation as conflicting with his beliefs. The family as he conceives it is mainly a relationship between parents and their children. He says, "Tiger has a mother and a father who love him dearly, and who have always supported him and always will. He is the top priority in the family. There is no bitterness between his parents, and there is no animosity. The only thing is that we live in separate places. My wife likes a great, big-ass house, and I like a small house. That's all." Even so, it's hard to believe that the division between Earl and Kultida doesn't go deeper than their preferences in accommodations—although they did stand together near the eighteenth green at the conclusion of the 2001 Masters, and they did spend that week in the same rented house in Augusta. There may be no animosity between them, but there doesn't seem to be much warmth, either. Maybe raising Tiger wore both of them out.

In 1997, when Tiger was just beginning his pro career, a regular golf partner of mine (and a retired schoolteacher) commented approvingly, "Tiger didn't grow up; he was brought up." I think that's true: Tiger's obsession with golf was obviously indulged by his parents, but the child wasn't spoiled. Almost from the beginning, he was made to take responsibility for his own aspirations. Starting when he was quite young, for example, he was put in charge of making the family's tournament-related travel arrangements. "When Tiger was a little boy," Earl later told a reporter, "he would check us into the hotel and I would check us out. Then, after a while, he'd do the whole thing. At the junior events, once he was grounded enough to handle everything at a golf tournament, he'd become the father and I'd become the follower, just for the tournament. He'd tell me what time we would get up in the morning. He'd decide whether we'd go out to dinner or eat in. Then, as soon as the last shot was hit, without either of us saying a word, we'd switch back." When Tiger was asked what he intended to study in school, he would say he hoped to major in accounting because he wanted to know how to keep track of the people who would one day keep track of his earnings. When he was still in his teens—according to John Strege, who wrote an unauthorized biography early in Tiger's career—he surprised his father one day by suddenly asking whether Earl would be able to live on a hundred thousand dollars a year; it turned out that he had been mentally crunching some numbers related to his future, and he wanted to be sure that his likely income as a touring pro would be sufficient to cover his parents' needs as well as his own. He went by himself to check out the colleges that recruited him, and he went by himself when it was time to enroll at Stanford, the one he ultimately chose. His parents resisted the urge to visit him until the spring of his freshman year because, Earl says, they wanted to strengthen his sense of independence. Earl says today that it was part of his plan all along to ease himself toward the sidelines of his son's life.

At the start of Tiger's career, sportswriters often wondered if he wasn't excessively dependent on his father, and whether that career might not derail if anything truly catastrophic happened to Earl. There were indications in those days that their continuing bond might be a crucial element in Tiger's performance, among them Tiger's poor showing in the 1996 Tour Championship, when Earl was in the hospital, and his ragged play in the 1997 Ryder Cup, in Valderrama, Spain, when Earl chose not to make the trip after being denied a place in the official entourage by the PGA of America (on the grounds that he was neither Tiger's spouse nor his significant other). But since that time, Tiger has demonstrated again and again that he is capable of standing on his own. He has also formed new personal relationships—among them his continuing friendship with the family of his neighbor and fellow tour player Mark O'Meara—that give his personal life something like the stability his parents once provided. It's easy to forget how young he was when his career began; he has grown considerably since then.

The real purpose of the Woods family's lifestyle, both parents have said, was not to turn Tiger into a professional golfer, but to strengthen his character. "Golf prepares children for life," Earl says, "because golf is a microcosm of life." According to Earl, the truly important lessons he imparted on the golf course had to do not with swinging but with things like honesty, etiquette, patience, and discipline—virtues for which golf provided handy talking points. (Golf is the only competitive sport, for example, in which the players call penalties on themselves.) Earl also stressed to Tiger that his athletic gift, if he continued to pursue it, would always entail outsized public obligations—not least of all because of his racial background. Tiger lived in a mostly white neighborhood in Cypress, California, and he attended mostly white schools, and he was sometimes harassed by bigoted bullies—one of whom tied him to a tree on the first day of kindergarten—but both his parents taught him to rise above such incidents and, in a phrase that Earl borrowed from the golf course, to "play through" them. Kultida urged him to be remorseless in competition, but she also steeped him in the Buddhist tradition in which she herself had been raised. Tiger absorbed these lessons and examples as readily as he had absorbed his father's swing. Earl told me that Kultida's spiritual teachings and personal example made a major contribution to Tiger's sense of "mental peace" during competition.

Tiger himself, in an article by Gary Smith in *Sports Illustrated* in 1996, was quoted as saying, "I like Buddhism because it's a whole way of being and living. It's based on discipline and respect and personal responsibility. I like Asian culture better than ours because of that. Asians are much more disciplined than we are. Look how well behaved their children are. It's how my mother raised me. You can question, but talk back? *Never.*"

If Tiger had been brought up by anyone else, would he be the player that he is today? The question is a tantalizing one, although we can never hope to untangle it. It appears that Earl and Kultida never took a false step in all those years in California, and that they provided their son with exactly what he turned out to need—competitive focus, celestial calm, immunity to intimidation, a cut-down one-iron—at every critical juncture in his development. But I sometimes wonder whether Tiger didn't in some sense "create" his parents as much as they created him. From the moment he climbed down from that high chair, he seems to have been phenomenally well equipped—temperamentally, emotionally, intellectually—to exploit the physical gift that he was born with. Is it outlandish to wonder whether part of his genius didn't lie in an ability to inspire his parents to conduct their lives in perfect harmony with his ambition?

3 *THE SWING*

LATE IN AUGUST 1996, Woods traveled to Pumpkin Ridge Golf Club, in North Plains, Oregon, to attempt an unprecedented third consecutive victory in the United States Amateur Championship. He was twenty years old and was about to begin his junior year at Stanford. Nearly four decades earlier, Jack Nicklaus had won the Amateur two times before turning professional, but his victories had been separated by a year. The last player to win the Amateur more than twice over the course of a playing career had been Bobby Jones, who won it five times between 1924 and 1930—but Jones never managed more than two titles in a row, and Woods was still two years younger than Jones had been when he won his first.

The U.S. Amateur consists of a thirty-six-hole

stroke play qualifying tournament—which yields a field of sixty-four players—followed by six rounds of elimination match play. Woods shot the lowest score—69-67—in the qualifying tournament, making him the top seed. He then comfortably beat four accomplished amateurs, J. D. Manning, Jerry Courville, Charles Howell, and D. A. Points. In the quarterfinal he faced Joel Kribel, who was a year younger than Woods and a fellow member of the Stanford golf team. Kribel got off to a strong start, and he led by two holes after the first nine. But Woods made a series of semimiraculous pars, and then he began to chip away at Kribel's lead. "You don't leave the door open for anyone," Kribel said later, "but especially not for Tiger. If you give him the slightest little opening, he's going to find it and make you pay for it." Woods did. While Kribel played the last eight holes in three over par, Woods made an eagle and two birdies, and closed out the match on the seventeenth green.

The following day, in the thirty-six-hole final, Woods faced Steve Scott, a sophomore from the University of Florida. Like Trip Kuehne in the Amateur final two years before, Scott got off to a commanding start; by the time the players broke for lunch at the end of the morning round, he led Woods by five holes. Woods needed not only to overcome this huge deficit, but also to avoid being mentally overwhelmed by the expectations of other people: sportswriters and television commentators all over the country had speculated at length about his chances of pulling off a triple. Woods insisted that he was focusing only on winning his matches, but how could he possibly shut his mind off entirely when his chances had been weighed repeatedly in nearly every newspaper in the country? The pressure had to be extraordinary. Scott, meanwhile, looked like the front page of tomorrow's sports section: his girlfriend was caddying for him, he was playing beautifully, and he seemed in every way as though destiny had tapped him for the job of reminding Tiger Woods of his mortality. STEVE SCOTT—GIANT KILLER —you could see the headline in your mind.

During the next few hours, though, Woods provided yet another powerful lesson for those foolish enough to bet against him. (That lesson has been thoroughly learned by sports fans now, but at the time it hadn't fully sunk in. Nowadays, golf spectators are far more surprised when Woods doesn't win than when he does.) He won the third, fourth, and fifth holes of the afternoon round—exactly what Scott had done during the morning round—and slashed his opponent's lead to two holes. He followed that streak by making seven threes on the ninth through seventeenth holes—three pars, three birdies, and an eagle. The final three, which he secured by sinking a forty-foot birdie putt on the thirty-fifth hole of the day, squared the match with one hole to play. Woods, through a long afternoon of sustained brilliance, had distilled the weeklong U.S. Amateur Championship into a one-hole tournament for the title.

Woods and Scott both parred that hole, a par-five, and sent their match into overtime. On the second extra hole, Scott made bogey while Woods tapped in a short putt for par. And that was that. "I was attempting to stop history, and I was unsuccessful," Scott said afterward. "You just have to wonder what it takes to beat this guy."

For quite a while, there had been a growing suspicion in the sports media that Woods would not finish all four years at Stanford. In response to questions from reporters, Woods offered a series of increasingly halfhearted reassurances about his intention to stay in school. That goal was right at the top of Kultida's list of priorities for her son, but how long could the world's best amateur remain excited about college golf? Woods had pulled off a triple victory in the Amateur, a record that will almost certainly never be topped, or even equaled. Now he faced the prospect of returning not only to his academic course load, which was heavy, but also to what is probably the most grueling competitive schedule in college sports: a ten-month season with tournaments all over the country. And Woods, inevitably, would want to continue to play in other events as well: not just the next year's Amateur, at which he would be the defending champion, but also the Masters, the U.S. Open, and the British Open (to which his Amateur title would earn him invitations), and a handful of tournaments on the PGA Tour, to which he would receive special invitations from the events' sponsors. (A player who has not yet qualified for the Tour can accept a limited number of these "sponsors' exemptions.") In 1961, Jack Nicklaus, with far less to distract him, had dropped out of Ohio State University after two and a half years in order to devote himself full time to golf. For Woods, remaining in school became close to a logistical impossibility.

In addition, Woods's potential value in the product endorsement marketplace had risen with each new triumph, to the point where continuing to play for free could be considered economically reckless. Even at this very early stage in his development as an athlete, Woods was a marketer's dream. His accomplishments were epochal, his potential was limitless, and he was young, intelligent, articulate, and multiethnic. At the Amateur, his gallery included Phil Knight, the chief executive officer of Nike, which was known to be deeply interested in making a deal. Now that Michael Jordan's basketball career was winding down, Nike needed another flagship athlete. Knight was also looking for an opportunity to get into the golf business in a big way; signing Woods would turn Nike instantly into a global force in golf.

Equipment endorsements mean more in golf than they do in other sports, because the game is not only watched but also played by its fans, whose clothing and equipment and travel purchases are heavily influenced by marketing expenditures. Ordinary hackers tend to outfit themselves with the clubs and balls and shoes and gloves and rain jackets and copper wristbands that they see their favorite pros using in the tournaments on TV, in the hope that a little PGA Tour magic will rub off on them. The ardor of such fans causes the golf equipment industry to behave in ways that don't seem to comply with the laws of economics. There is far more competition among golf ball manufacturers today than there was just a few years ago, for example, but that increase in competition has paradoxically led to an increase in ball prices, not to a decline. Why? Because the only way for one manufacturer to distinguish its products from those of another is through blitzkrieg-style marketing programs centered on endorsements by the game's top players, and those programs are phenomenally expensive. To make their own products seem special, the big manufacturers compete with one another for the opportunity to throw money at the game's superstars, and those endorsement fees push up the prices of the balls that you and I buy. (A dozen premium golf balls costs just four or five dollars to make, but often sells for more than fifty dollars.) We ordinary golfers may grumble, but an astonishing number of us nonetheless pay up, because we want to believe that we can change our lousy luck simply by changing our equipment. And because we buy into the illusion, the competition for top players can be intense: when David Duval switched his allegiance from Titleist to Nike last winter, Titleist sued.

Not surprisingly to anyone who had done the arithmetic, Woods's announced intention to finish college didn't last long. On the Wednesday following his Amateur victory, at a press conference in Milwaukee—the site of the next stop on the PGA Tour—he announced that he had made up his mind. "Well, I guess it's 'Hello, world,' huh?" he said, announcing that he would now compete as a professional. Within a few days, golf fans learned that "Hello, world" had not been a charmingly boyish (if supremely self-confident) ad lib, but was the theme of a big new Tiger-centric advertising campaign by Nike, which had agreed to pay Woods forty million dollars over the next five years.

It was by no means clear at that point that Nike would receive value for its money. Woods's performance in PGA Tour events up to that point, as an amateur, had been underwhelming. His opponents in his storied Amateur matches had been not the best players in the world but "college students and car dealers," as one sportswriter said; now he would be going up against guys who played golf for a living. The list of past Amateur champions includes a handful of players who went on to become highly successful on tour—among them Hal Sutton, Phil Mickelson, and Justin Leonard—but it also includes an awful lot of guys you never heard of. And in addition to the difficulty of playing at a new level, Woods faced the challenge of maintaining his competitive focus under an almost inconceivably high level of public scrutiny. Jack Nicklaus has said that he had the advantage of beginning his career in relative obscurity, without the burden of immediately having to live up to huge expectations; Woods hadn't taken a swing as a professional yet, and he was already the most famous golfer in the world.

Some wondered also whether Woods hadn't stacked the odds against his own success by turning pro so late in the Tour's 1996 season, with just seven tournaments remaining. Woods would easily be able to obtain sponsors' exemptions to play in all seven of those tournaments—the PGA Tour permits players to receive exactly that many in a year—but he wasn't leaving himself much room to find his way for the following year. In order to earn full playing privileges for 1997, he would need to either win a tournament or finish among the top one hundred and twenty-five players on the Tour's money list for the year—something that Stuart Appleby, an extremely promising young Australian player (who has since won three times on the American tour and twice been a member of the international team in the President's Cup) would fail to do despite competing in thirty events. If he finished among the next twenty-five, he would have the right to accept an unlimited number of sponsors' exemptions in tournaments with openings. If he finished worse than a hundred and fiftieth, he would have to enter the Tour's notoriously demoralizing qualifying "school," which is actually a grueling six-round tournament for aspiring Tour players—an outcome he very much wanted to avoid.

(By turning pro, too, Woods would be giving up a guaranteed invitation to the 1997 Masters, since he had qualified by winning the U.S. Amateur but would no longer be an amateur and therefore would no longer be entitled to play. After Woods had not only qualified for that Masters by winning on tour but had also won it, with the lowest total score ever shot in the tournament, Jack Stephens, who was the chairman of the Augusta National at the time, told me that he had originally worried that Woods's giving up his Masters invitation by turning pro was the equivalent of "taking points off the scoreboard in a football game." Then he laughed, and said, "I guess Tiger knew better than I did.")

But Woods didn't seem worried about the challenge that lay ahead of him, and neither did his father. When sportswriters asked Earl if he really thought his son could finish in the top hundred and twenty-five, he was dismissive of their doubts. "Giving Tiger seven chances to win a tournament," he said, "he's going to win one of them"—a comment that prompted much chortling in the press tent.

As it turned out, though, Tiger didn't play in seven events; he played in just six. And he didn't win one of them; he won two.

o   o   o

WOODS'S FIRST TOURNAMENT as a professional was the 1996 Greater Milwaukee Open. "I'll never forget," he said three years later. "In Milwaukee I teed up my golf ball, put my club down, and thought, I'm fine, no big deal, I can do this. I took the club back, and I swear it felt like it took about fifteen seconds for that club to get to the top of my swing. It was so heavy. I have never experienced anything like that in my life. But I got through it. And, luckily, my ball went out there three-twenty, and I made birdie."

Woods shot 67, four under par, in the first round— a very respectable debut. But Nolan Henke (62), Bob Estes (64), Duffy Waldorf (65), and Mike Sullivan (66) were among a dozen players—none of them superstars and none of them the owners of forty-million-dollar Nike endorsement deals—who shot lower scores that day. Woods was now competing in a universe in which even the journeymen are capable of going low. He fell back on Friday with a 69, and put himself out of the tournament on Saturday with a 73. He finished with a 68, including a hole-in-one, and ended up in a nine-way tie for sixtieth place out of the seventy-six players who had made the cut. His first tournament earnings check was for $2,544, or about one and a half percent of the amount he would most likely need to earn before the end of the season in order to finish high enough on the money list to win his card for the following year. (Woods, despite being a millionaire many times over at this point, loved that piddling first tournament check; in his view, it was the first money he had truly earned by playing golf.)

Here's how Woods's next few weeks went:

• In his second tournament, the Bell Canadian Open—which was shortened to fifty-four holes after play was twice interrupted by rain and wind on Saturday—he finished in eleventh place, six shots off the winning score. On Sunday, in miserable weather, he shot 68, which was the low round of the day.

• A week later, at the Quad City Classic, in Illinois, Woods led the tournament after three rounds, by one stroke over Ed Fiori, who was forty-three years old and one of the shortest hitters on tour. Fiori played with Woods on the final day, outscored him by five shots, 67 to 72, and ended up with his first Tour victory in fourteen years, and the fourth of his career; Woods finished in a tie for fifth place. His downfall had come early in the final round, when he made a reckless quadruple-bogey after building a three-shot lead. "I will tell you one thing," Woods said afterward, "I will learn a lot from this."

• A week later, at the B.C. Open, in Endicott, New York, rain again caused the final round of the tournament to be canceled. Woods finished in a tie for third, just three strokes out of a playoff with Fred Funk (the eventual winner) and Pete Jordan.

• The following week, in late September, Woods withdrew from the Buick Challenge. His decision not to play in that event created general consternation. The tournament's sponsors were upset, because Woods's absence would mean a steep drop in ticket sales, and the sponsors of the Fred Haskins Award— which is given each year to the best college golfer— were upset because Woods, who was that year's winner, had also decided not to attend their award banquet, which was scheduled to be held during the tournament. Woods later had to make things right with the Haskins Commission, by agreeing to appear at a rescheduled banquet, but he definitely needed a break. "I can't ever remember being tired when I was twenty," Tom Kite said, expressing a sentiment that was shared by many Tour players. But neither Kite nor any other Tour player had ever experienced the kind of pressure that Woods had been enduring for more than a month now. Counting his week at the

Amateur, he had been playing full-bore since August—twenty-three rounds in thirty-five days—and he had spent nearly every waking moment during that period surrounded by golf fans, sportswriters, television commentators, official and unofficial advisers, agents, hucksters, sponsors, and others who wanted nothing from him but every remaining unscheduled moment of his time. Tom Kite, at any age, had never experienced anything like that.

• During the first week of October, feeling refreshed after a week at home in Florida, Woods arrived in Las Vegas for his fifth tournament as a professional. The Las Vegas Invitational is played on three golf courses and includes five rounds instead of the usual four. Woods had a mediocre first round but steadily worked his way up through the leaderboard during the week, and finished Saturday's round in a tie for seventh, four shots out of the lead. He shot 64 the next day, and held the lead briefly by himself before being tied by Davis Love III, who was in the final group. Their playoff lasted just one hole: Love teed off first, hitting driver, and then Woods hit three-wood, leaving himself a slightly longer shot to the green and thereby securing for himself the age-old match play advantage of being able to attack first. He put his ball close to the hole, and Love didn't, and Woods was the winner. Gary Van Sickle, in the next week's *Sports Illustrated,* wrote, "Golf, as we know it, is over."

In his six-week march to victory as a professional, Woods recapitulated the rising arc of a standard first-rate PGA Tour career: it was as though he had grown a full year older and more experienced with every week, between one Thursday and the next. That first week was like a promising young player's maiden season on tour: he felt his way around and committed a variety of predictable errors, but he made the cut and earned enough money to cover his expenses—a solid start. In the second week, he seemed a full year more mature, and he came close to finishing in the top ten. In his third week, now another year older and stronger, he learned what it was like to hold and lose a lead—the aspiring player's traditional trial by fire, and the experience Tom Watson has described as every future winner's compulsory initiation: learning to lose—and finished in the top five. In his fourth week, with another year's worth of emotional growth under his belt, he finished third in a shortened event, and knew that if bad weather hadn't canceled the final round he might well have gone on to win. The next week, exhausted, he succumbed to the pressure of his burgeoning success, burned out, and backed away from the grind of the Tour—the good player's inevitable dark night of the soul. The next week, renewed and reinvigorated, he won. And there it was: an entire top-flight professional career, with all the necessary intermediate steps, compressed into little more than a month.

As a player, Woods has always seemed to have an uncanny ability to evolve at light speed, rising from plateau to plateau without bothering to stumble up the steps in between. The sportswriter Tom Callahan told me, "One very interesting thing about Tiger is that he never does a thing in any area until he gets there, at which point he immediately becomes the best there is. When he was a junior player, winning all those USGA junior cups, he didn't do anything spectacular in tournaments against good older amateurs. He never popped up and had a big moment in the U.S. Amateur, for example—until the instant he won his first, when he suddenly became the best amateur in the world. And during the period when he was winning his three Amateur championships, he didn't do a thing in PGA Tour events, even though he played in quite a few of them, starting in 1992 at Riviera. In other words, he wasn't at all like Sergio Garcia, who contended in and won pro events as an amateur, or like Phil Mickelson, who actually won a PGA Tour event when he was in college. Tiger never even got a call—until the moment he arrived, when he was suddenly better than everybody else. The same was true with the majors. Before the 1997 Masters, he had had just one good round in a major tournament—at the 1996 British Open, Royal Lytham and St. Annes, where he shot 66 in the second round. Now he's got the scoring record in all four of the majors, and people are surprised if he doesn't win. That's not the way it's been for most of the big guys. Nicklaus probably should have won the U.S. Open as a twenty-year-old amateur—he finished second instead. Tiger's career hasn't been like that. He has never done a thing at any level until the instant he got there, when he suddenly did everything. He has never been fully engaged until the moment he became fully engaged."

And, as if anyone needed proof that he was for

real, he added an exclamation mark to his amazing maiden season by also winning the first event of the following year, the 1997 Mercedes Championships, giving him a nearly inconceivable three victories in his first nine starts as a pro.

o   o   o

I FIRST SAW WOODS in person at Augusta National Golf Club, in Augusta, Georgia, during the week of the 1997 Masters Tournament. Late one afternoon before the Masters itself began, I was standing near Augusta National's first tee when Woods emerged from the clubhouse to play a practice round. The sun was low in the sky, many spectators had gone home, and there were few players left on the golf course. I didn't see Woods at first, but I quickly guessed that he was near, because the crowd loitering between the clubhouse and the first tee suddenly convulsed. At that moment, he was the biggest athletic celebrity in the world, and people who had seen him only on television were jostling for a glimpse. He was moving fast, and he was encircled by guards. "Tiger! Tiger! Tiger!" The ardor of those fans I can describe only as ferocious. Their supplications sounded almost angry. The distance between the roped sanctuary of the clubhouse terrace and the roped sanctuary of the first tee measured just a few dozen yards, but for a moment that narrow strip of lawn seemed potentially impassable. Woods's face floated expressionless among the grimaces of his protectors.

When the competition began on Thursday, Woods made a disastrous start. He played the first nine holes in forty strokes, four over par. I was wandering in and out of Augusta National's spacious press building while he was playing those holes, and there was a feeling in the air that Woods's early run of bogeys constituted the athletic equivalent of the bursting of a speculative bubble. This brilliant young player had come awfully far awfully fast, the feeling went, and here, in his first major tournament as a professional, he was having his comeuppance—and he was having it at the Masters, the tournament that Nicklaus, with six victories, had made the bulwark of his career.

Just when Woods seemed to be playing himself out of the tournament, however, something remarkable happened. "I knew what I was doing wrong," he said afterward, "so it was getting out of that and trusting the motion from there." He made birdies at the tenth, twelfth, and thirteenth holes, and then, with a six-foot putt at the fifteenth, he added an eagle. He made another birdie, on the seventeenth hole, and he nearly made one more on the last, with a putt that just missed. He ended the day at two shots under par, just three strokes out of the lead, having played the second nine holes in ten strokes fewer than the first. Only three players, out of a field of eighty-six, stood ahead of him. "It was a tough day initially," he said, "but I got through it."

For most of his professional career, Woods has been at or near the top of the ranking in a statistical category that the PGA Tour calls "bounce back," which is a measure of how likely a player is to make a birdie or better immediately after making a bogey or worse—an indication of the player's resilience and ability to refocus following a disappointment. Woods "bounces back" roughly a third of the time, a remarkable achievement. He also has a pronounced ability to follow a good round with an even better one—to bounce forward. In the second round of the Masters, he shot 66, reaching the halfway point of the tournament with a three-shot lead.

For the third round, Tiger was paired with Colin

Montgomerie, who had played well enough the day before to have shared the lead for a short time early in his round. He was now tied for second. Montgomerie, who is Scottish, had been the best player on the European PGA Tour for several years, and he had been a star of European Ryder Cup teams throughout the 1990s. He has never won a tournament in the United States, but he had come close a few times and had done well in several major tournaments. He was especially optimistic about his chances that week in Augusta. In an interview before the first round, he spoke with great self-confidence. "I'm a better player than I was last year," he said. "I've improved every year, so I'm a better player than I was in '96. I'm hitting the ball right to left with ease. And although I didn't putt well at [the Players Championship, the week before], I feel I'm actually putting quite well." In fact, he said, in practice he had putted Augusta's fast, undulating greens "better than I ever have before."

Playing side by side with Woods on Saturday, however, was a transforming experience for Montgomerie. He shot 74—a score that ordinarily wouldn't have been disastrous at that stage in a major tournament, except that Woods shot 65 and thereby increased his lead over the field to nine strokes, and his lead over Montgomerie to twelve. When their round was over, Montgomerie was taken to the press building for a postmortem, as the top players always are; he looked frazzled and discouraged as he stepped onto the stage, and he didn't wait for anyone to ask a question.

"All I have to say is one brief comment today," he began. "There is no chance. We're all human beings here, but there's no chance humanly possible that Tiger is just going to lose this tournament. No way."

"What makes you say that?" a reporter asked.

Montgomerie looked at the reporter with palpable incredulity. "Have you just come in?" he said. "Or have you been away? Have you been on holiday or something? Or have you just arrived? Sorry. What do you mean 'what makes you say that'?"

The reporter, abashed, explained that Tom Kite had just chastised the press corps for prematurely declaring Greg Norman the winner of the previous year's Masters. In 1996, Norman had begun the final round with a six-stroke lead—an edge that most players, reporters, and spectators had believed to be impregnable. But Norman's game disintegrated under the pressure of Sunday at the Masters, and Nick Faldo, who played with him in the final pairing, ended up winning by five shots. Kite had just warned the reporters not to be so hasty this time.

"This is very different," Montgomerie said. "Faldo is not lying second, for one thing. And Greg Norman's not Tiger Woods." He was clearly shaken by what he had witnessed at close quarters. "I had appreciated that he hit the ball long and straight," he said, "and I had appreciated that his long irons were very accurate. I had not appreciated how well he putted. When you add it all together, he's nine shots clear. And I'm sure that will be higher tomorrow."

A reporter reminded Montgomerie that, the day before, Montgomerie himself had said that Woods might not yet be seasoned enough to withstand the pressure of holding the lead in a major tournament.

"He is," Montgomerie said bluntly.

There wasn't much more. "My game doesn't really take much talking about today, really," he concluded. "It was quite poor. I played the par-fives badly. I'll just let Tiger Woods come in. He's waiting."

And Montgomerie got up and left. In his encounter with Tiger Woods, he had crossed from the first stage to the second stage in the process described by Emily Dickinson as "First Chill—then Stupor—then the Letting Go." In the fourth and final round he shot 81, a dismal score, which left him in a tie for thirtieth place. When he finished, he looked as though his body had been drained of blood.

o   o   o

PICKING MY WAY through a crush of fans, I followed Woods as well as I could at various times during that Masters, which he ended up winning by a record-breaking margin of twelve strokes. (He broke or tied twenty-five other Masters records that week, too—among them the overall scoring record, which had been set by Nicklaus in 1965 and tied by Raymond Floyd in 1976.) Two moments in particular stand out in my memory. The first occurred roughly midway through one of Woods's rounds. In the hope of gaining a better vantage point from which to view some of the tournament, I had climbed to the top of a tall press tower, which stood alongside the eighteenth green and was used mainly by photographers. At one point, Jack Nicklaus was putting on the eighteenth green, directly below. This was his thirty-ninth appearance in the tournament, but no one in the tower was watching him; we all had our backs turned, and we were leaning over the tower's rear railing. We were trying to get a glimpse of the eighth green, which was more than a quarter-mile away, on a hilltop beyond a stand of tall pine trees, because that was where Woods was playing at that moment. Two other writers and I shared a pair of binoculars. We couldn't see Woods, but we had been told that he had reached the green of that par-five in two shots. Then we heard a roar, and knew that something big had happened. A few moments later we heard another roar, as the tally of Woods's birdies on the main scoreboard was increased by one. Nicklaus, meanwhile, had finished his round and departed to record his score.

The second moment that sticks in my memory occurred on the thirteenth hole on Friday. That hole is probably the most storied par-five in the world—the third of the three holes known together as Amen Corner. Its sloping fairway curves to the left along a tributary of Rae's Creek, the far side of which is flanked by tall pines. Woods hit a big drive around the corner that day, leaving himself a perfect angle to the green. He hit his second shot with an eight-iron—an amazing club selection, considering that Ben Hogan often used a three-iron just to lay up on that hole—and I was standing in the gallery on a direct line beyond him when he did. Viewed from my position, Woods's ball seemed to take off almost vertically, and in exact alignment with the flag. The ball also traveled an ungodly distance for an eight-iron shot, and it took what seemed like minutes to return to earth. As it descended, it appeared to me to have a chance to land in the hole. Instead, it ended up fifteen or twenty feet beyond. Woods made that putt, for eagle, and thereby improved his score by two more strokes in relation to par.

Weekend golfers who attend professional tournaments for the first time are almost always struck by the breathtaking quality of the pros' shots, and they end up realizing sadly that professional golf and weekend golf, despite superficial similarities, are very different games. This truth was driven home for me for the first time at the 1993 Ryder Cup, which was held at a club in northwest England called the Belfry, not long after I'd taken up the game myself. At one point—with the help of a media armband, which let me walk inside the ropes—I was following Fred Couples and Paul Azinger, who were playing a four-ball match with Nick Faldo and Colin Montgomerie. On the sixth hole, Couples pushed his drive into the rough on the right side of the fairway. That shot left him with about a hundred and seventy-five yards to the hole, which had been cut in the back left corner of an elevated green, and there was a stand of small trees directly in his line. He chose a five-iron. As I crouched in front of the gallery, almost close enough to Couples to reach out and touch his shoe, he hit a languidly stratospheric fade that soared far above the trees, nearly disappeared against the sky above the left side of the green, turned back toward the flag, and ended up maybe twelve feet from the hole. (He would later sink the putt, for a birdie.) My jaw dropped. Even more impressive than the parabolic trajectory of the shot was the apparent lack of effort that Couples had expended to produce it. I suddenly understood that I always had been and always would be a chopper.

By the time I went to the 1997 Masters, I had watched many other touring pros play brilliant golf, and I had even played casual rounds with a few of them, so I had no remaining fantasies about my own abilities in comparison with theirs. But some of Woods's golf shots during that tournament seemed almost as different from an average pro's shots as an average pro's shots would seem from mine. They belonged in a category of their own—and the difference is obvious to the pros as well. David Feherty, a former Tour player from Ireland who now works mainly as a television commentator and a writer, says, "I played for a living for twenty-five years, and I've played with just about everybody, and I think I can say now that Tiger has hit virtually every truly great shot I've ever seen. As we speak, he is deleting some of my greatest memories and replacing them with his. He simply does things other golfers can't do. He's like the Heineken in the commercial: he refreshes the parts other beers cannot reach."

o   o   o

WOODS'S DOMINANCE at the 1997 Masters was so complete that some observers later concluded Augusta National itself needed an overhaul. In *Golf World* the week after the tournament, Tim Rosaforte wrote, "It's time to fire up the bulldozers, buy the strip malls on Washington Road"—the busy street that borders the eastern edge of the club's property—"and re-design the place. Grow the rough. Add some forced carries. Dig some pot bunkers. Bring in Pete Dye, the railroad ties and the island greens. Tell Tom Fazio to quit tinkering and get serious: Augusta National needs the full-metal overhaul. It needs U.S. Open vegetation, or it's going to be a one-man tournament until Tiger Woods gets bored and decides to take up baseball."

Rosaforte was partly being facetious, but the view he sketched is widely held. There is a common feeling among golf fans that not only Augusta National but competitive golf itself needs to be "Tiger-proofed." Holes need to be lengthened, people say, and landing areas need to be tightened, or else Woods will ruin the game by making the world's great tournament courses look like Putt-Putts.

Such feelings are understandable, but the proposed solutions are mostly illogical, since lengthening a golf hole merely increases the advantage held by Woods or any other long-hitting player. If you or I had to go head-to-head with Tiger Woods, our only realistic chance of keeping up would be on a very short hole, where we might get lucky; on a very long one, Woods's advantage in length would be insurmountable, and his edge would increase as the distance did. On a hundred-yard par-three, for example, Woods and I might both hit the same club off the tee (although Woods undoubtedly wouldn't swing as hard as I would have to), and I might get lucky and make a birdie—or even a hole-in-one; on a six-hundred-and-fifty-yard par-five, in contrast, Woods would have a decent chance of reaching the green in two shots, while I would have to hit three or four perfect ones just to get close. Tour players face the same problem. Woods's biggest scoring advantage over other pros is on the longest holes, the par-fives and the long par-fours; adding yardage to those holes would merely increase his edge. On an eight-thousand-yard golf course, the only golfer in the world who wouldn't have to breathe hard would be Tiger Woods.

Woods has sometimes seemed to have more trouble on relatively short holes than he has on extremely long ones. At the 1997 Masters, one of the few holes that he didn't overwhelm was the third, which measures just 360 yards and is one of the two shortest par-fours on the course. Many players hit irons from the tee, and most are usually left with short irons or even wedges for their approaches. During the second round, on Friday, Woods decided to try to overpower the hole, by hitting his driver from the tee. I was standing in the gallery behind him when he swung, and I had an exhilarating view of his ball, which looked like a small white cruise missile as it screamed up the tree line on the right side of the fairway. The ball flew low and curved slightly to the left, and it came to rest just short of the green, perhaps fifteen yards from the front edge. Woods then hit a poor chip, and he ended up making his only bogey of the day. In doing so, he demonstrated that, paradoxically, the only way to "Tiger-proof" a golf hole—if such a thing is even possible—is probably to shorten it. (Woods, characteristically, has sorted out his early difficulty with Augusta National's third hole. In the 2001 Masters, he birdied it in both the first and second rounds, playing the hole in two under par for the tournament.)

Curiously, length is the only one of Woods's numerous competitive advantages that significant numbers of sportswriters, Tour players, and golf fans seem to consider unfair. In the 1997 Masters, Woods's four rounds included just a hundred and seventeen putts—an average of 1.63 a hole—but no one suggested that Augusta National's greens ought to be made more severe in the hope of reducing his supremacy with his putter. The reason may be that golfers tend to think of good putting as a learnable skill (and therefore one that they themselves could acquire if they were willing to work at it), while 350-yard drives are the work of the devil. This way of thinking is widespread in the golf world; players who chip and putt well are said to have good imaginations, while players who hit the ball a long way are thought of as brutes. Woods complicates such assessments by consistently being better in all departments than almost anyone else.

o   o   o

WOODS'S GOLF SWING is so powerful that it is difficult to capture on film. For many years, *Golf Digest* has published detailed photographic sequences that anatomize the swings of the game's best players—sequences that are descended in spirit from the studies of running athletes and galloping horses which were

made in the late nineteenth century by the photographic pioneer Eadweard Muybridge. Since 1973,
the magazine's photographers have shot their swing
sequences with a high-speed camera called a
Hulcher, which was originally developed at the request of a government agency to take stop-action
photographs of missiles. The camera can shoot hundreds of high-quality images at a rate as fast as sixty-
five frames a second—plenty fast enough to break a
golf swing into its constituent parts.

Woods performed for the Hulcher a few months
after his Masters victory. (He has an ongoing contractual relationship with *Golf Digest;* his first agree-
ment with the magazine, which he signed in the
spring of 1997, was said to be worth a million dollars
a year and to measure his personal commitment in
minutes. He reupped in 2000.) The camera
recorded fifteen driver swings from five different angles. When the prints came back from the lab, the
magazine's editors discovered that only five frames
among the hundreds taken during the entire shoot
had captured Woods's swing at the approximate moment his clubhead came into contact with the ball—
a problem they had never had before. "With other

Tour players we almost always get a picture of impact with every swing," Roger Schiffman, the executive editor, said. When Woods makes his normal swing, the head of his driver moves at about a hundred and twenty miles an hour—a good fifteen miles an hour faster than the clubhead of a typical touring pro, and about thirty miles an hour faster than the clubhead of an average amateur. Between one Hulcher frame and the next, Woods's driver traveled through roughly two hundred degrees of arc, meaning that a ball sitting unthreatened on the tee in one frame would be long gone by the next. The magazine's technical editor, Art Chou, said, "Due to Tiger's acceleration through the ball, it was a fluke that the Hulcher recorded impact on even one of Tiger's swings."

That *Golf Digest* swing sequence was photographed two days before the start of the 1997 Western Open, which Woods went on to win. "When he saw the pictures later," Schiffman told me, "he said, 'No wonder I won.' He said his swing looked almost perfect." It was quite a surprise, therefore, when Woods decided not long afterward that his game required a major overhaul. With the help of Butch Harmon, his teacher, he spent more than a year taking apart his "almost perfect" swing and putting it back together.

◦   ◦   ◦

THE EYES OF NONGOLFERS glaze over when golfers fret about their swings, as they do when offered the least opportunity. If you play golf, though, you understand the fascination. The golf swing may be the most frustrating motion in sports. It's all angles and levers and timing and voodoo, and because it starts from a dead stop and is directed at a stationary object, it permits, and even encourages, a dangerous level of conscious interference. Most athletic actions work best when the attention of the athletes executing them is focused somewhere else—on a rapidly approaching tennis ball, for example, or on the footsteps of a furious linebacker—but golf is a highly self-conscious game. As a result, golf instruction often veers in the direction of pop psychology, and the advice offered in countless books, magazines, videos, infomercials, television shows, and week-long swing schools can begin to seem oracular. ("Swing easy as hard as you can"; "Don't be tight"; "Don't be loose"; "You can play well with a bad swing as long as you make an even number of errors.") Golf is so unnerving that longtime players are susceptible to a host of bizarre and virtually incurable mental disorders, among them a putting problem known as "the yips," and a calamitous swing breakdown known as "the shanks"—a condition so devastating that many golfers superstitiously refuse to utter its name.

The great tennis player Pete Sampras said in an interview with Bob Verdi in 1999 that his tennis swing hadn't changed in ten years. Golfers, in contrast, fuss constantly with their fundamentals (as Sampras does when he plays his second favorite sport). At the Ryder Cup in 1993, I stood by the driving range for half an hour while the British player Nick Faldo, who was probably the best golfer in the world at that time, worked on swing minutiae with his teacher, David Leadbetter. Faldo would address a ball, then sweep his club halfway to the top of his backswing and freeze; Leadbetter would modify the position of Faldo's hands by an inch or so; Faldo would read-dress the ball, then sweep his club halfway to the top of his backswing and freeze; Leadbetter would modify the position of Faldo's hands by an inch or so. They repeated this exercise again and again and

again. (The real proof that golfers are mentally un-
balanced was provided not by Faldo and Leadbetter,
but by me: I stood there and watched. And took
notes!) For most players, this sort of incessant med-
dling is necessary yet perilous. Faldo himself suffered a swing collapse a few years ago, and he is still
trying to rediscover his old touch. Many average
golfers are afraid to take lessons, fearing that their
habitual swing, though disastrously flawed, might
collapse altogether if they permitted anyone to fid-
dle with it.

Woods's dissatisfaction with his swing in 1997
seemed, to an outsider, almost reckless—especially
because it concerned a problem that most golfers
could never conceive of as a problem. I saw an example of this dissatisfaction once in a tournament on
TV. Woods had driven his ball beautifully on a par-
four, leaving himself just a short iron to the green—
an easy shot. He swung, and his ball soared through
the air, and, sure enough, it ended up just a few feet
from the hole. (He would later sink that putt, for a
birdie.) But Woods reacted as angrily as if he had just
bounced his ball off a car in the clubhouse parking
lot.

He later revealed what had bothered him: he had intended to play a fade—that is, a shot that starts left of the target and curves back toward it, to the right. At some point during his downswing, however, he sensed that his club was in the wrong position in relation to his body, so he manipulated his hands in such a way that the clubhead rolled over at the bottom of his swing, imparting side spin to the ball in the opposite direction and causing the shot to curve from right to left instead—a shot known as a draw. Because of the speed of his swing, and the time it takes for electrical impulses to travel back and forth through the human nervous system, that sort of midcourse correction is almost impossible to comprehend. In any event, despite the end result, Woods didn't like having to rely on his hands to twist his club into the right position, so he decided the time had come to tighten up his swing. That process took more than a year, and it coincided with the only relative dry spell in his career thus far—a period, which ended late in 1999, during which he won only a tournament or two. Since then, he's been red hot.

I won't bore you with the details of how Woods and Harmon did it—and the details are definitely boring—but the process included hitting thousands upon thousands of practice balls, enduring countless hours of tedious drills, and adding several brick-sized slabs of muscle to what was already a virtually fat-free physique. Woods has always loved to practice, and he is a fascinated and deeply analytical observer of his own swing. "He is the best student I ever had," Harmon says. "He is like a sponge—he soaks up information, and he always wants to learn and get better." That notion is deeply disturbing to a typical weekend golfer, who half believes that a new five-hundred-dollar driver or a single magical golf tip might turn out to be the key to a fabulous second career, on the Senior PGA Tour. It's also disconcerting to other Tour players, who had more than enough trouble with the old Woods—the one with the allegedly terrible swing. Now they have to deal with a Woods who not only can improve, but wants to. Harmon describes his student as "a work in progress," and they both say that the Woods we have seen so far is only seventy-five percent as good as the Woods they both believe we will see at some point in the future—and probably sooner rather than later. "He can get a lot better," Harmon told me. "Scary thought. He can become more consistent in all areas of his game, and his scoring will improve as he becomes more familiar with the golf courses of the Tour."

"I've worked countless hours," Woods himself said shortly before his Oklahoma exhibition. "People have no idea how many hours I've put into this game—and they don't really need to know, either—but I've put in a lot of time and a lot of effort. My dad always told me that there are no shortcuts, that you get out of it what you put into it, and that if you want to become the best you're going to have to be willing to pay your dues."

(Incidentally, one reason Woods and Harmon have such a successful working relationship, according to Woods, is that Harmon has a similarly severe work ethic and has also devoted "countless hours" to what he does. "Butch loves to watch film," Woods said at the 2000 U.S. Open. "He'll sit there for hours on end, analyzing, critiquing, and trying to find something in my swing that he can see when I'm not swinging well, or things I'm doing right when I am swinging well. It's that hard work that you give confidence to; you can feel that he's always there for you. He's doing the right thing. And there's never been a time I've ever questioned him. We've talked things through, but there's never a doubt that he and I are always on the same page.")

In the summer of 2000, I asked Earl if there was any aspect of his son's development as a golfer that had surprised him—any part of it that he hadn't foreseen. He said there wasn't—but then, upon reflection, he corrected himself. "There's one little area," he said. "That's the timing of it. I was thrown off by two years, because he came out of college two years ahead of time. As a result of that, one of the critical areas in which he still has room to improve is his physical maturity. You see, he is not physically mature yet. I had thought that spending four years in college would give him time to grow, and then he would come out and in about a year he'd be mature physically, and then he would take off. Well, it's been three years now, and he is still maturing. He put on fifteen pounds last year, and you can imagine what another fifteen pounds will look like at the end of this year. He fights his distance control all the time, because he hasn't finished growing. He is still gaining yardage.

The rest of them aren't ever going to hit the ball any farther than they can hit it right now, but Tiger just keeps getting stronger. Hell, he wakes up in the morning and he has another three to five yards with his irons. Where does that come from?"

4 *BEING TIGER WOODS*

I ONCE WATCHED Tiger Woods walk into a large room filled with well-dressed, well-behaved, well-to-do people, who were on hand to attend a banquet at which Woods was the guest of honor. They pretended to ignore him for a little while, as polite grown-ups will usually do when they are trying hard not to act silly in the presence of a celebrity. But then one person, somewhat bashfully, approached Woods and asked him for an autograph, and then another asked, and then another. And then—you could see heads turning all over the room—the crush began. Uncapped indelible markers loomed in Woods's face from all directions. Strangers gripped his shoulder or grabbed his hand. Parents pressed reluctant children forward to the front of the crowd. From six feet away, disposable cameras fired their flashes at Woods's eyes. Many of the people who still managed to hold themselves back appeared suddenly anxious: shouldn't I be asking for an autograph, too? They kept their distance but couldn't take their eyes off Woods. Restraining myself took a surprising (to me) amount of effort—and I'm a supposedly cynical sportswriter.

I don't think any of the people at that party were planning to run home and sell their Tiger mementos on eBay, so it wasn't naked greed that prompted them to ruin Woods's evening. Encountering a very famous person creates churning emotions in most of us. We want to consummate the meeting somehow, to embed it in reality. Tiger Woods, for almost all of us, is someone who exists only on television and in the sports pages and in magazines; now, suddenly, here he is in the flesh—catch him before he gets away! A signature on the back of a dinner menu lends tangibility to a moment that otherwise seems evanescent.

If you don't count the times I've dutifully asked various friends to sign copies of books they'd written, I've asked for just two autographs in my adult life: Muhammad Ali's and Paul McCartney's. (I stood in line at a book party in New York in order to ask Ali to sign my copy of a book about him; I talked to McCartney briefly in Paris, at a fashion show featuring a collection designed by his daughter Stella, and, after another grown-up boldly asked him for an autograph, I swallowed my pride and asked him to sign a program for my children.) But there have been many other occasions when I have only barely managed to resist an overpowering urge to stick a pen in the face of someone famous. And there have been times when I have acted even dumber than that.

A few days before the 2001 Masters, I was standing in the golf shop of the Augusta National Golf Club when Justin Leonard, whom I had never met, came in looking for change for a hundred-dollar bill. It happened that I had just been to the bank, so I gave him five twenties, and we exchanged the usual lame jokes about counterfeit currency. There was nothing notable about that hundred-dollar bill; Leonard hadn't signed it or drawn a funny picture on it, and I hadn't won it from him on the golf course. It was just an ordinary piece of currency which had briefly ridden around in the wallet of the twenty-fourth best golfer in the world. And yet for more than a month I couldn't bring myself to spend it. When I told my son about it, he asked to see it, and we spent a surprisingly long time handing it back and forth and looking at it and saying that it was cool. In the middle of a round of golf a couple of weeks later, I told two golf buddies about it, and they asked to see it, too, and then, later, when I realized that I didn't have much other cash in my wallet, they wouldn't let me use it to pay for my share of lunch, insisting that I borrow money from them instead. I finally did spend it—at a hardware store, on seventy-five dollars' worth of spring cleaning supplies—but only because I had left my Visa card at home. Handing that bill to the salesperson made me almost wince with regret. (If the bill had come from Woods, I suspect I might have reshelved my cleaning supplies and gone home.)

In a strange way, I think, the brevity of my encounter with Leonard probably contributed to my irrational feelings about that hundred-dollar bill. Two days before, I had actually played golf with Jim Furyk—the twelfth best golfer in the world—but hadn't bothered to save even our scorecard. Maybe that encounter seemed "real" in a way that my encounter with Leonard did not, and it therefore didn't cry out to be documented with a ridiculous souvenir. Maybe spending time with a famous person makes his or her celebrity seem less numinous.

Mementos from the famous also give us a delusive community with our heroes. This is the sports fan's most precious fantasy; it's what causes us to take personally the victories and defeats of athletes who don't know we exist. The delusion can be extraordinarily powerful. In 1977, Jack Nicklaus served as the presenter at the Gold Tee Award ceremony of the Metropolitan Golf Writers Association, in New York. On his way in to the banquet, he was stopped by a man who seemed to know him very well. Nicklaus couldn't place the face—was this guy a business associate? a relative of his wife's? someone he had known in college? The man suddenly sensed that Nicklaus didn't know who he was, and he looked deeply hurt. "At the U.S. Open two years ago," he prompted. "You were on the first tee—and I was the guy who yelled, 'Go, Jack!' "

o   o   o

THIS IS PRETTY MUCH what Tiger's life is like whenever he ventures outside the protective boundary he has erected around his private life. People are generally better behaved in his presence now than they were back in 1997, but they still intrude. Many more years will have to pass before he will again be able to, for example, stroll unmolested through an airport terminal, or eat an uninterrupted meal in a randomly selected restaurant. Or maybe he will never again be able to do those things; maybe our ardor has pushed him forever beyond the outer limits of a normal-seeming existence.

Nicklaus never had to put up with anything like that at the comparable moment in his career. When he was beginning to turn the golf world upside-down, the prevailing mood among golf fans was one of mild animosity, because Nicklaus was threatening the hegemony of the game's most popular player ever up to that point: Arnold Palmer. One of the many impressive accomplishments of Woods's young career is how well he has stood up to the public onslaught and, in fact, how successful he has been at creating and defending a private space in which he can live something like a regular life. He does not give individual interviews to print reporters, except on rare occasions here and there, and then only briefly. He does not discuss certain subjects (such as his weight-training regimen, for some reason, and his girlfriend of the moment). He does not sign golf balls. Reporters still grumble about having to live with restricted access; the first two paragraphs of *Sports Illustrated*'s cover story about his 2000 U.S. Open victory concerned not the tournament but Woods's refusal to be interviewed on the practice tee by reporters from two different television networks. But having limited access to Woods is probably a blessing at this point. What could anyone possibly ask him that he hasn't been asked a thousand times already?

Sportswriters complain about being frozen out, but when they do find themselves with opportunities to ask him questions—as they do in press tent interview rooms—they tend to cover the same tired ground again and again. No wonder Woods sometimes cannot hide his impatience. In a group interview before the 1999 Memorial Tournament—which Woods went on to win—the first question from a reporter was "How about an opening statement?"

"About what?" Woods asked frostily.

The moderator pitched in. "What's the question?"

"You'll have to tell me," Woods said.

"Let me ask you this, then—" the hapless reporter began again.

"There you go," Woods said.

"You've talked about every facet of your life," the reporter continued. "Shooting 40 at age three—that's still amazing to me."

"Forty-eight," Woods said.

"The bio says 40."

"I shot 48 when I was three from the ladies' tees at my own course. But I had every ball teed up. I had to sweep it off the ground at the time."

"A memorable round for you?"

"I don't know many people who can remember when they were three years old."

No doubt this sportswriter, like most sportswriters, complains about being denied one-on-one access to Woods. But here was a moment when he had an opportunity to ask Woods anything he wanted, and look what he came up with. Is it any wonder that Woods doesn't rush at the opportunity to hang out with us whenever we decide we need a quote? For most of us, suddenly being granted an hour of face time with Woods would be a frightening experience (aside

from the press tent bragging rights that would ac-
company such apparent intimacy with the star). At
this point in his career, what could anyone think to
ask him that he hasn't been asked a thousand times
before? *Uh, Tiger, how come you're so great?*

The sportswriters' frustrations are understandable; some of Woods's achievements are nearly in-
comprehensible, even to grizzled veterans of the golf
beat, and we all wish that Woods would help us out by
stepping forward more often with a reasonable explanation, or at least a printable cliché. In the interview room at Augusta National following the 2001
Masters—which Woods won by two strokes, making
him the first golfer ever to hold all four of the game's
professional major titles at the same time—a reporter asked, "When Pete Rose got his record-
breaking hit, he looked in the sky and said he
thought he saw his father. Was there any part of your
life that you thought of when you got emotional on
the green, any moment of gravity for you?" Woods's
answer got a big laugh: "No." You could easily see
what the reporter was hoping for: a poignantly heart-
warming quote about Earl or Kultida or the
Almighty—an Oprah moment, like the sudden ap-

pearance of that rainbow over the final green at the 1997 PGA Championship as Davis Love III, aided by memories of his late father, finally won his first major. But Woods wasn't playing the cliché game.

Despite occasional moments of obvious irritation, however, Woods has lightened up considerably with sportswriters since that chilly pressroom interview at the 1999 Memorial—even when the sportswriters can't think of anything truly interesting to ask. In the first round of the 2000 U.S. Open, for example, he was paired with the Swedish golfer Jesper Parnevik, who is known not only for his golf and his dietary habits (among them a penchant for volcanic sand) but also for various sartorial flourishes. On that day, Parnevik had worn a bright orange shirt, which, like most of his golf shirts, didn't look very much like a golf shirt. Toward the end of the group press interview after that round, Woods was asked what he had thought of the orange shirt. The reporter who asked the question was clearly looking for a joke—a little touch of levity with which to decorate his story—and Woods, instead of dismissing the question, cheerfully offered three. "Well, he was noticeable out there," he said. Pause. "You could see him in the fog, that's for sure." Pause. "He was our beacon, so no one would hit into us." That's quite a change, and it's one that has to be the result of conscious effort.

°   °   °

A FEW MONTHS BEFORE Tiger Woods was born, Dan Jenkins wrote a magazine article called "How Bob Drum and I Invented Arnold Palmer." The title was partly meant to be funny, and partly not. The article concerned the era—which by 1975 was already over—when professional golf was something like a joint production of the men who played it and the men who wrote about it for newspapers. "Writers have golfers, you know," Jenkins wrote. "And golfers have writers. In a way, I suppose, a lot of us thought of ourselves as a modern-day version of O. B. Keeler, who had Bobby Jones." Keeler was Jones's adoring hagiographer, who lovingly reported on nearly every phase of Jones's competitive career. Jones would probably still be a mythic figure in the golf world today if Keeler had never come along, but it was Keeler who first struck the reverent tone that has

characterized writing about Jones ever since. He
spotted Jones early and made him his life's work.
And he made up most of the quotes.

Jenkins and Ben Hogan were both from Texas, so
Hogan belonged to Jenkins. If Drum (a Pittsburgh
sportswriter closely associated with Latrobe, Pennsyl-
vania, native Palmer) needed a quote from Hogan,
he was as likely to go to Jenkins as to the man himself.
"If I didn't have any yet," Jenkins explained, "I would
invent one. If Drum didn't like it, he would yell, 'I
read that in a Herbert Warren Wind *book*, you rotten
son of a bitch. Gimme something fresh.' Ultimately,
together, Drum and I would come dangerously close
to making Ben Hogan out to be a standup comedian
in *The Pittsburgh Press* and *The Fort Worth Press*." Jenkins and Drum gave Palmer the same treatment, often
leaving the man himself to read his own remarks for
the first time in the following day's paper. According
to Jenkins, they also helped to inspire Palmer's
epochal come-from-behind victory in the 1960 U.S.
Open, at Cherry Hills, by virtually goading Palmer
into marching out and shooting 65 in the final
round. "As we loitered on the fifth tee," Jenkins
wrote, "Arnold took the Coke in a paper cup out of

my hand and sipped on it. He took a pack of cigarettes out of my shirt pocket and lit one." And so on and so on.

Stories like that bring tears to the eyes of aging sportswriters; the era it evokes faded out as television faded in. The Tour in the good old days wasn't the media-saturated corporate juggernaut that it is today. Purses were small, and the players and the correspondents traveled together, drank together, and kept one another's secrets. If a big-name pro was cheating on his wife, everybody knew it but nobody wrote about it.

When televised tournaments were few and coverage was limited, print reporters were the principal conduit between players and fans. Palmer was golf's first television star, but most of what golf fans knew about him at the peak of his career came from guys like Jenkins, whose dispatches turned the game into an ongoing narrative and made a golf tournament or a player's career a story with a beginning, a middle, and an end. Television increasingly provided the pictures, but the first glimpses it offered were brief. For many golf fans, the Masters didn't really end with the television broadcast on Sunday of tournament week;

its true conclusion came weeks later, when Herbert Warren Wind's endlessly unhurried account of the action finally appeared in *The New Yorker.*

Those days are gone now; television has eliminated the need (and the patience, on both the giving and receiving ends) for leisurely mediation between performers and spectators. A golf fan with an Internet connection and a decent cable television package can easily learn more today about the lives of minimally successful Tour players than a golf fan thirty or forty years ago could ever have hoped to know about the game's biggest stars. Anyone who watches golf on television is inundated with raw information. We know the players' putting problems, we've studied their swings in slow motion, we've heard the considered professional judgments of their instructors and their sports psychologists, we've seen pictures of their children and their wives and their ex-wives. But this seeming intimacy is partly an illusion. Television is a wall as well as a window.

Today, even the people who cover golf for newspapers do much of their work by watching TV. At big tournaments, sportswriters don't need to set foot on the course itself; they can stay inside the press tent and watch the action on a great big screen. To step out onto the course risks missing a crucial shot witnessed by every golf fan watching from a living room at home. At the Masters—where the press tent is actually a huge, permanent building equipped with networked laptop computers, an instantaneous scoring system, and Krispy Kreme doughnuts—reporters don't even need to leave their seats. They can watch not only the regular television broadcast but also nine separate live closed-circuit feeds, one from each of the last nine holes. They can use headphones to listen to player interviews taking place elsewhere in the building, and they don't need to take notes, because printed transcripts are provided moments after the interviews end. (If you read tournament accounts in more than one newspaper, you routinely find that the same quotes appear over and over.) At the 1995 U.S. Open, which was played at Shinnecock Hills Golf Club, on Long Island, a rumor circulated among reporters that a distinguished older sportswriter, who was famous for covering major tournaments from inside the press tent, if not from the bar at his hotel, had contracted Lyme disease. "The only way he could have Lyme disease," another writer said, "is if you can catch it from limes."

Actually, thanks to television and the Internet, the press tent itself is almost superfluous. Important interviews at major tournaments are sometimes carried live on the Golf Channel, and transcripts of even unimportant interviews are posted promptly on the Web site of the Golf Writers Association of America and elsewhere. Various Web sites provide hole-by-hole scoring details as well as the sort of statistical, biographical, and historical information that reporters used to have to dig for. Sportswriters could cover the Masters from a basement in Dubuque and none of their readers would necessarily be the wiser.

°   °   °

TIGER WOODS BEGAN to be noticed in a big way by the general golfing public during the thirty-six-hole final match of the United States Amateur Championship in 1994, the match in which Woods came back from five down with twelve holes to play to beat Trip Kuehne. The most dramatic moment in the match occurred on the thirty-fifth hole, when Woods made a bold birdie and took the lead for the first time in the match. When his putt dropped, Woods pumped his fist, made a menacing face, and strutted across the green. That fist pump—which became quite familiar to golf fans in succeeding years—attracted a good deal of criticism, as did some of Woods's other emotional demonstrations, such as slamming down a golf club after a bad shot or uttering a string of oaths not usually heard on network television. A woman on an airplane once asked me if Woods was really "just a spoiled brat." I said that I believed he was very nearly the opposite, and that his parents and teachers and friends would undoubtedly back me up. She was reacting to some emotional outburst that she had seen on TV; to her, Woods looked like a tantrum-throwing child.

Other pros made similar remarks. In 1999, Arnold Palmer said, "I think that frown all the time, and that slamming the club down doesn't do anything for his game or the game. He's got the world in his hands. All he has to do is enjoy it and laugh, and enjoy the ability that he has to the fullest extent. He's not convincing anybody of anything when he slams a club down. They know he's good. He's proven that."

When I first read Palmer's remarks—which have been quoted many times since he made them, and are usually characterized as a "mild reprimand"—I laughed, because I had recently been working my way through the Augusta National Golf Club's collection of movies and television kinescopes of old Masters Tournaments, and I had been enjoying some vintage footage of Arnold Palmer in his playing prime. In that footage Palmer paced and scowled and hitched up his pants, and although I don't think the camera ever caught him slamming down a club it did catch him slamming down quite a few cigarettes. At the peak of his talents, in other words, Palmer was a very different character from the genial senior statesman who brought tears to our eyes as he took that final trip over the bridge on the eighteenth hole at St. Andrews during his last British Open, in 1995. Back in the years when he was the world's best player, Palmer burned adrenaline like rocket fuel, as Woods does now. The emotions he felt and often displayed on the golf course in those days weren't distractions from his talent; they were part of it. Palmer had the world in his hands, too, and one of the reasons he did was that he wasn't just smiling and waving to the crowd.

"It's interesting how people say golf needs more emotion," Woods said not long after Palmer made his remarks. "Then we start expressing emotion on the golf course, and we're crucified for doing it because it's not the right kind of emotion. You can't have the good without the bad."

Sportswriters and sports fans have criticized Woods for caring too much about money (as we did when he let the PGA Tour know that he felt the Tour was exploiting his image without adequately compensating him); yet we have also criticized him for not caring enough about money (as we did when he said, in an early interview with Curtis Strange, that "second place sucks"—a comment that was interpreted not only as arrogant but also as professionally naive*). Our problem may be that we are able to think of his life and career only in roughly the same

---

*Woods isn't the first great golfer to be unimpressed by being a runner-up. Jack Nicklaus, at the age of twenty, after finishing second by two strokes to Arnold Palmer in the 1960 U.S. Open, grumbled, "I didn't win. Nobody ever remembers who finished second at anything." The great players really don't like second place.

terms in which we think of our own: a hundred million dollars would make us lose interest in our jobs, and second place sounds plenty good to us. Meanwhile, Woods seems unfazed. "Probably the single thing I most admire about Tiger Woods," Hal Sutton said late last year, after Woods had signed a new endorsement deal with Nike, "is that he can sign a $100 million deal today and wake up tomorrow with the same desire to be the best in the world."

○   ○   ○

WHEN WOODS SAID, "You can't have the good without the bad," he was underestimating his own ability to rein in his emotions. He has scaled back the famous fist pump, and he seldom really unwinds anymore, although there have been notable exceptions. At some level, though, the state of his emotions is not inseparable from the rest of his game.

"I think everyone gets mad on the golf course," the sportswriter Tom Callahan told me. "Even Catholic priests say bad words on the golf course. The thing about Tiger is that he lets it go instantly. He has that bolt of anger, and then four yards away from it he's smiling and talking to Steve Williams, his caddie. I was once talking to Billie Jean King about John McEnroe, and I asked her how it was possible that McEnroe, an intelligent person, could be up six-love, six-love, five-love, forty-love in a match, and then the linesman would blow a call and McEnroe would go off like a roman candle. I said you want to shout at him: 'Hey, don't you think you're going to win a point in the next hour and a half?' And she said, 'He can't think that way.' She said he lives in what she called the Universal Moment, where the only thing that matters is the shot at hand. That's the only thing he cares about, and it's the only thing he's thinking about—the shot at hand. I think she was right about McEnroe, and what she said applies to Tiger, too."

Woods's biggest outburst came at the 2000 U.S. Open at Pebble Beach. Bad weather caused a suspension of play on Friday, forcing Woods and a number of other players to finish their second round on Saturday morning, before teeing off for their third. On the eighteenth tee, Woods hit what he later described as "probably the worst shot I hit all week"—a pull-hook into the Pacific Ocean—and unleashed a burst of profanity that was vividly audible on television. "Well, it was the heat of the moment," Woods said later. "I'm one of those guys who play pretty intense, and, unfortunately, I let it slip out." (Woods's blue streak did take place very early in the morning, before the regular round of the day, at a hour when a player might be excused for not having a television audience foremost in his mind.)

He was widely criticized for the outburst, but other observers felt that reaction was unfair, or hypocritical. David Feherty said, "People were saying, What kind of a role model is this? That just amazes me—that people struggle so hard to try to find something negative to say about him. You know, I was sitting there with my kids, and I was watching him on TV, and one of my kids said, 'Dad, Tiger said a bad word.' And I said, 'You're right. He did say a bad word. And I will expect you to say exactly the same bad word if you ever find yourself in the same position. But that's the only set of circumstances in which you are allowed to say that word.' And he said, 'Okay, Dad, that's fine.' Now, that's parenting. But I was right. When you consider the things that other athletes do—the end zone gloating, and the throat slashing, and the coach choking—how can you criticize Tiger Woods in any way for his behavior, which is exemplary to say the least? I mean, this is a game in which you are meant to lose your mind on occasion."

For those capable of suspending dismay at the particular words Woods used, the incident provided a telling insight into his competitive mind. An instant after his explosion, Woods's mood was transformed. He had put his bad drive entirely out of his mind, and he managed to make a bogey on the hole—giving him the equivalent of a birdie on his second ball. And his display of anger (and subsequent total restoration of his composure) proved that he wasn't coasting. He had already built a preemptive lead in the tournament, which he would go on to win by an almost inconceivable margin of fifteen strokes, but if you saw only his reaction to that tee shot you might have guessed that he had just blown his first shot on the first hole of a sudden-death playoff. Woods plays each shot as though it were the most important. In a tournament in which no other player seemed capable of giving him much of a fight, he remained as focused and as intense as if the entire PGA Tour were breathing down his neck.

Woods's occasionally explosive intensity on the golf course isn't a blemish on his competitive personality; it's an inseparable part of it. He is gradually learning to keep a lid on some of the outward manifestations of that intensity, but he will always burn inside. Nicklaus has always been the same way (although I don't recall ever hearing him on TV using words that Woods used that morning at Pebble Beach). A couple of years ago, I interviewed Nicklaus briefly in the tournament headquarters building at Augusta National, and the whole time we were talking the hard look in his eyes said, "I could ask better questions than that—you want to play questions?— I'll take you on in questions." He wasn't misbehaving; he was just being Nicklaus. No one becomes the best in the world in any competitive field without harboring a certain level of inward ruthlessness. Only with enormous effort did Bobby Jones learn to refrain from having tantrums on golf courses when the game wasn't going his way. "In my early years," he wrote in *Golf Is My Game,* a collection of instructional articles and autobiographical sketches that was published in 1960, "I think I must have been completely intolerant of anything less than absolute perfection in the playing of any shot. I often heard Grantland Rice tell of seeing me break a club after hitting a pitch that stopped two feet from the hole, simply because I had not played the shot as I had intended." Jones gradually grew more successful at suppressing such displays, but the raw emotion was always there. "To the finish of my golfing days," he also wrote, "I encountered golfing emotions which could not be endured with the club still in my hands."

We sports fans tend to think of great athletic accomplishments as ennobling triumphs of the human spirit. But the will to win is a darkly complex internal force, and it is one that in almost any other human context would seem far less admirable than it does on the playing field, and not at all humane. Spouses or siblings or office mates or neighbors who treated each other with anything like the same determination to dominate that Woods and Nicklaus and other great champions show their opponents would seem like monsters. For an athlete in competition, remorselessness is a virtue, and empathy is a fatal flaw. The last thing an athlete can afford to do in the closing moments of some great contest is to become concerned about the feelings of the rest of the field.

At a "media day" press conference with Woods about a month before the 2001 U.S. Open, a reporter asked a question that approached this complicated issue. "When I play golf," the reporter said, "I want to be nice, be gentle to the other players. What do you recommend if I care to be a true golfer—a really good golfer?" I think the reporter was trying to tempt Woods into talking about the cold heart of the champion—about the competitor's need to be able to do what Kultida supposedly urged her son to do back in his junior golf days: when you have an opponent down, step on his neck. But Woods, in his response, seemed not quite to see the point of the question; his answer was nothing more than locker room boilerplate: "To be a good golfer," he said, "I think it basically goes down to your work ethic—having a good work ethic, a good foundation, some good fundamentals. But, more important, just going out there and busting your tail on the range, the putting green, the chipping green, and really learning how to play the game of golf—and then applying what you've done on the range and on the practice putting and chipping green in play. When you play with your weekend buddies, I don't think that's the easiest thing to do, but it's something I've learned how to do. I think it's been very beneficial to me."

We fans feel exalted when we watch great athletes perform, but our reaction is at least partly paradoxical, because great athletes are the ultimate narcissists. Their focus is inward, and it is purely selfish. The "work ethic" that Woods talks about is really a rarefied species of self-absorption. No matter what we may think about the virtues of hard work, there's something unnerving about the image of Ben Hogan hitting practice balls until his hands bled. The payoff for Hogan, finally, was in public performance, but the source of his need to win was dark and deep and invisible to his own eye, and it had nothing to do with us.

5 *CHANGING GOLF*

TIGER WOODS has changed almost everything there is to change about golf. The conventional wisdom among sportswriters used to be that the PGA Tour had become so deep in talent that no modern player could hope to dominate it the way Palmer or Nicklaus or Watson did in the 1960s and 1970s and 1980s, or the way Snead or Nelson or Hogan did in the 1930s and 1940s and 1950s. Now, though, Woods becomes the favorite in any tournament simply by signing up, and professional golfers all over the world have begun lifting heavier weights, eating healthier food, and going to bed earlier, in the hope of becoming good enough to be considered second best. "He's in their heads," Tom Callahan says. Callahan recalled the corrective eye surgery that Woods had in 1999. "The first thing he said afterward was, 'The hole looks bigger.' Now, if you're Davis Love, is that what you want to hear?" More than a few pros once viewed Woods as dangerously overhyped; nowadays, like most of the rest of his awestruck admirers, they tend to stop what they're doing and watch—perhaps thinking ahead to a day when they'll be able to brag to their grandchildren that they once got personally whomped by "the Chosen One" (as the tour player Mark Calcavecchia called him at the 2000 British Open).

Woods has caused the world's best players to reevaluate their understanding of their own talent. In the 2001 Masters, Phil Mickelson—who was ranked No. 2 in the world at the time—began the final round one stroke off the lead and, playing alongside Woods, remained in contention until the last couple of holes. But during that final round he made four bogeys (along with six birdies) and ultimately finished in third place, three strokes back. Those four bogeys—along with two double-bogeys he had made earlier in the week—haunted him when the tournament was over.

"If I'm going to win with Tiger in the field," he said

during a post-round interview, "I cannot make the mistakes that I have been making. I've got to eliminate those somehow. I may be able to make one or two, but I can't make as many as I made all week, from double-bogeys on twelve and fourteen earlier in the week, to four bogeys today that were really not tough pars." Mickelson had made his final-round bogeys on the fourth, sixth, and sixteenth holes, which are all par-threes, and on the eleventh, which is a long par-four. (Tim Dahlberg of the Associated Press once wrote that Mickelson's "history in majors is littered with bad swings at inopportune moments.") "I just think that, mentally, I'm not there for all seventy-two shots," Mickelson continued. "I feel like I'm just slacking off on two or three, and just kind of letting momentum take over, and not really thinking through each shot. And it's cost me some vital strokes."

The key word in Mickelson's statement was "somehow," because it captured the amorphousness of the problem that the world's great players face when they set their minds on competing with Woods. Short of going back in time and growing up all over again, perhaps with Earl Woods in charge of their development program, what can they possibly do to raise their performance to a consistently higher level? Mickelson, in his interview, was critiquing the mental side of his game, but Woods has prompted him to wonder about his physical skills as well. In another post-Masters interview, he said that as a player he had always relied heavily on "feel"—a gifted golfer's code word for natural athletic talent. Before Woods began to dominate the tour, Mickelson said, he had been able to succeed at the highest levels without being overly analytical about his technique. Through the 2001 Masters, Mickelson had won eighteen times on the PGA Tour. Nonetheless, he realized that if he was to have a hope of consistently competing at Woods's level, he was going to have to adopt something like Woods's ultra-focused work ethic—and, potentially, to remake his own swing in something like the way that Woods had remade his. Instinct was not going to get the job done.

Mickelson was talking about far more than working harder in the fitness trailer, or hitting more balls on the driving range, or spending more time on the practice green. At his extraordinary level of accomplishment, marginal improvements in long-term performance are usually gained only with enormous difficulty, if they can be gained at all. Beginning players can lop ten or twelve strokes off their handicap simply by improving their grip or stance, or by learning to line up putts more accurately, or by mastering the correct technique for hitting a ball out of a bunker. For the top players, though, real gains over long periods are hard to come by. Mickelson's implicit goal is to improve his scoring average, when he's playing at the top of his game, by something like a half-stroke a round. Mathematically, the difference seems almost trivial, and yet for a player at Mickelson's level the effort might involve spending a year taking his swing apart, only to find himself unable to put it back together again; or he could discover that concentrating on swing mechanics over an extended period of time had had a deleterious effect on other, formerly reliable parts of his game. One of the truisms of golf instruction is that focusing on technique during competition, as opposed to focusing on where the ball needs to go, is often fatal; but here was a great player concluding that it may be time for him to focus on technique.

"It's no secret," Earl says. "The formula is hard

work, imagination, creativity, and talent. And the average PGA Tour player can work hard and do everything else, but they don't have the talent level. That's what separates Tiger. And that's what these guys are striving to catch up to. They work hard, and they work hard, and they work hard—and then they look down at the end of the driving range, and who's that down there working? This little dark figure? Wait a minute, his skin's too light—it's not Vijay Singh. No, that's Tiger. And they realize that, Oh, no, he's outworking me, too. Then they think—Oh, God, the talent. That's when they realize that they aren't going to catch up."

Increasing the gap between Woods and the rest of the field has been Woods's ability to maintain a nearly impermeable barrier between his competitive mental state and the normal spectrum of human emotion. His parents continue to be an extremely important part of his life, but he has demonstrated repeatedly that he no longer depends on their direct encouragement to maintain a competitive frame of mind. (When he walked past his mother on the way to the first tee at the 2001 Masters, he was so focused on the tournament that he betrayed no glimmer of recognition.) He has real friends, with whom he maintains a social life, but he isn't married, and he doesn't have children. For about three years, he did have a steady girlfriend—a law student and former college cheerleader named Joanna Jagoda—but they broke up in late 2000. To an outsider, Jagoda had seemed like an ideal companion for Woods: she kept a very low profile at the golf events she attended, she didn't give interviews, and her friends were discreet with reporters. According to press tent scuttlebutt, the cause of their split was Woods's lack of interest in making their relationship permanent. Earl Woods has said that Tiger won't be a complete human being until he has married and raised a family of his own, as Jack Nicklaus did, but Tiger has shown no eagerness to settle down. As a result, he doesn't have to endure the emotional and personal conflicts experienced by some of his closest rivals. Mickelson—who wore a beeper during the 1999 U.S. Open because his wife was due to give birth to their first child at any moment, and who had announced that he would drop out of the tournament if she went into labor, even if he was leading at the time—once said that the best thing he and his fellow PGA Tour members could do to improve their chances against Woods would be to set him up with dates.

                    ○   ○   ○

WOODS'S EFFECT ON other professional golfers hasn't solely been to raise the Tour-wide paranoia level. By playing phenomenally well, Woods has inspired other golfers to play better than they thought they could. One of Woods's best friends on Tour is Mark O'Meara, who lives near him at a wealthy gated community called Isleworth, in Windermere, Florida. (Isleworth is also the home of Ken Griffey, Jr., among other athletic celebrities; Michael Jordan and Shaquille O'Neal are both members of Isleworth Country Club.) O'Meara, who turned forty in 1997, isn't quite old enough to be Woods's father or quite young enough to be his big brother, but he and his wife, Alicia, have informally adopted their young neighbor, and they have contributed an important source of personal stability to his life. O'Meara and Woods play golf together and fish together, and the week before the 2001 Masters they got up before dawn to fly to Augusta for an early and private practice round. O'Meara has given Woods the benefit of his twenty years' experience as a professional, and Woods, in turn, inspired O'Meara to play some of the best golf of his life. In 1997, O'Meara won the AT&T Pebble Beach National Pro-Am by a single shot, holding off a spectacular late charge by Woods himself, who birdied the last three holes. "It's great for Mark," Woods said in an interview after that tournament. "We live about a three-wood away from each other. He and I talked about going head-to-head, and, lo and behold, we did today." The next year, O'Meara, at the age of forty-one, won both the Masters and the British Open—the only two major titles of his career. An important ingredient in both victories was the new level of determination and self-confidence that O'Meara had acquired through his friendly rivalry with his neighbor: Tiger rubs off on people. A veteran sportswriter contends that O'Meara's two majors probably ought to be added to Woods's total, on the theory that O'Meara never would have won them if Woods hadn't pushed his game to a higher level. "The thing our grandchildren are going to wonder," he said, "is how Mark O'Meara managed to win two major championships in the Tiger era. He obviously didn't make friends with Tiger in order to become a better player, but their relationship is the best thing that ever happened to his golf game. His career was pretty average before Tiger came along. Then, for a while there it looked like he could win everything."

Even touring pros whose personal relationship with Woods doesn't extend beyond the locker room have gained enormously from their professional association with him. Prize money on the Tour in 1996, the year Woods turned pro, added up to a little more than $69 million; the total purse in 2001 was $180 million, or more than two and a half times as much. (Woods's own Tour earnings in 2000—$8,286,821, a single-season record—exceeded the PGA Tour's total purse no further back in history than 1975.) Much of the increase has come from the growth in television revenues, a gain for which Woods is single-handedly responsible. "Myself and my wife thank Tiger every day," the tour pro Dennis Paulson said earlier this year. "I've made about a half million more in the last year and a half than I would have, because of him."

One effect of the increase in wealth on tour is that

no player who is remotely in contention at the upper
levels of the game can claim to be distracted by
money worries anymore. There is so much money in
purses and endorsements and other income opportunities for the better players—not just the best players—that the threshold of true financial security has
been pushed far down the money list. The situation
is quite different from what it was, for example, at the
first Masters, in 1934, where only the first twelve
places paid anything at all, and the total purse
amounted to just five thousand dollars. (To raise
even that small sum, the members of the Augusta National Golf Club had to pass the hat among themselves at the last minute.) The Tour's leading money
winner during the year before that tournament was
Paul Runyon, who won nine events and had total
earnings of less than sixty-five hundred dollars.

As his career has blossomed, Woods has sometimes
felt that the Tour's management has not shown sufficient appreciation for his contribution to the pros-
perity of professional golf. In the fall of 2000, after a
period of growing dissatisfaction, he made public remarks in which he accused the Tour of, in essence,

taking him for granted. Speaking of Tim Finchem, who is the Tour's commissioner, Woods told Tim Rosaforte and John Hawkins of *Golf World,* "The only time he talks to me is when he wants me to do something for him. To play in this tournament or that tournament—it's not like he comes up to me and asks me how I'm doing." Finchem, who can come across even in casual conversations as arrogant and impersonal, clearly realized that he'd better patch things up in a hurry with the game's golden goose. Shortly afterward, he and the Tour's chief legal counsel sat down for a private summit conference with Woods, who attended the meeting with his agent and his father. The issues they discussed reportedly included the ownership of Internet rights related to Woods and his career—rights that Woods has indicated he hopes to exploit himself in a variety of ways over the coming years. After the meeting, which Woods described as highly satisfactory, Finchem seemed subdued but pleased, or maybe relieved. Woods's contentment level has a direct and powerful influence on the financial well-being of a large and growing group of people—among them Tim Finchem, whose total compensation in 2000 would have placed him in the top five on that year's Tour money list.

°   °   °

IN ADDITION TO RAISING the financial stakes, Woods has changed golf's public image, which has suffered for decades from the game's suburban association with saddle shoes, cigars, and miniature electric cars. "Golf was called a wussy sport when I was growing up," he said in Oklahoma. "You weren't supposed to play it unless you were a wuss." No longer. Twelve-year-olds who used to dream only of becoming professional basketball players now sometimes decide that they might like to give the PGA Tour a try, too, at least in the off-season. (In many television markets, the third and fourth rounds of the 2000 U.S. Open earned higher Nielsen ratings than the National Basketball Association's championship series, which overlapped the tournament—an epochal achievement for golf, especially since the only suspense remaining in the Open by that point was how many records Woods was going to crush.) Tubby middle-aged hackers now stand a little taller at cocktail parties, because Woods, miracle of miracles, has made golf seem kind of cool. When a teenage checker at my local grocery store discovered that I played a lot of golf, her eyes lit up, and she asked, "Have you met Tiger?"

When I called home from the 1997 Masters to check in with my family, my son, who was nine, informed me that he had just hit all my practice balls into the trees across the road from our house. He had never shown much interest in golf before that moment, but he had watched some of the Masters on TV, and Woods's performance had seduced him. He immediately gave Woods an exalted place alongside Michael Jordan in his small personal pantheon of sports heroes. A week later, I visited the normally semideserted driving range at my little local golf club and found that all the parking places and all the teeing positions had already been claimed, in some cases by golfers I didn't recognize. "It's been like this since the Masters," a friend of mine said. Some of those hitting balls were starry-eyed kids, but plenty of grown-ups were flailing away as well. Of course, their urge to hit balls was at least slightly irrational, since Woods's example is one that mere mortals can't hope to emulate. But Woods's record-breaking performance had awakened something in all of them—and the effect has continued. When I started playing golf, in the early 1990s, our course, which has just nine holes, was often empty on weekdays, even during perfect weather. A self-employed golf buddy and I, taking advantage of our flexible work schedules, used to do most of our playing during the week, when we sometimes shared the place only with the guy mowing the greens. Now those days are gone, and Woods is most of the reason.

Most astonishing of all, Woods has taken the most shameful theme of golf's long history—its legacy as a decadent pastime for white people with too much time on their hands—and turned it inside out. For a hundred years, golf in America has stood as a potent symbol of exclusion and racial intolerance. It is still overwhelmingly a white man's game, but Woods has cracked it to the core, and there is no doubt that when he eventually retires he will leave the game in a very different condition from the one in which he found it.

American golf got off to a surprisingly promising start where race is concerned: a black man named John Shippen played in the second United States

Open, which was held at Shinnecock Hills Golf Club in 1896. Shippen had worked on the crew that built the course, and he later became first a caddie and then an assistant to the club's head professional, a Scotsman named Willie Dunn, and eventually a professional himself. In fact, Shippen is credited by some with having been the first American-born golf pro. Another player in the 1896 Open was Oscar Bunn, an American Indian, who also worked for Dunn. A group of British players, the dominant force in competitive golf of that era, threatened to withdraw from the tournament if Shippen and Bunn were allowed to play. The president of the United States Golf Association, Theodore F. Havermeyer (whose name is preserved on the trophy awarded to winners of the U.S. Amateur Championship), replied that Shippen and Bunn would be allowed to play even if they turned out to be the only players remaining in the field. The British players backed down. Shippen finished the first round (of two) in a tie for the lead; he finished the tournament in a tie for fifth place, and won ten dollars.

Shippen played in four more Opens—and he served as the head professional at a number of clubs, among them Maidstone Golf Club, during the first half of the twentieth century—but his participation in the 1896 Open turned out to be the high-water mark of enlightened race relations in American golf for many decades to come. Between 1934 and 1961, the constitution of the Professional Golfers Association—the direct predecessor of the modern PGA Tour—explicitly limited that organization's membership to "Professional golfers of the Caucasian race." The Caucasian-only clause was not some esoteric historical artifact; the rule formalized a policy that had always been understood, and the PGA bothered to put it on paper after discovering that a light-skinned black man named Dewey Brown had worked as a club professional since 1928. The PGA dropped his membership the year the Caucasian-only rule went into effect.

For the next twenty-seven years, the PGA methodically fought efforts by black players to overturn or circumvent the rule. In 1948, for example, three talented black players—Teddy Rhodes, Bill Spiller, and Madison Gunther—successfully entered the Richmond Open, a PGA event in California, but were prevented from playing after the association learned that they were black. The three men sued; the PGA kept the case out of court at the last minute by agreeing to permit black players to compete in its events (though not to drop the Caucasian-only membership clause). The settlement was a hollow one, however, and the PGA essentially ignored it. In 1952, for example, Rhodes, the boxer Joe Louis, the black pro Charlie Sifford, and a black amateur named Eural Clark were allowed to play in a qualifying round for that year's Phoenix Open, but they were hardly welcomed with open arms. Calvin H. Sinnette, in a book called *Forbidden Fairways: African Americans and the Game of Golf,* writes, "After being denied use of the locker-room facilities, Louis, Rhodes, Sifford, and Clark were sent out as the first group of the morning in the qualifying round. At the first green, they were greeted by the revolting sight and smell of human excrement that someone had surreptitiously placed in the cup."

The PGA didn't amend its constitution until it was forced to do so—and the pressure for change did not come from any white pros of that era, who were apparently happy with their world the way it was. In

1960, Stanley Mosk, the attorney general of California, informed the organization that it would no longer be allowed to conduct tournaments in that state if it continued to discriminate against black players. The PGA responded by announcing that it would thenceforth hold its California events only at private clubs. But Mosk warned the PGA that he was prepared to take further steps if the organization attempted to evade his ruling, and, late in 1961, the PGA finally gave in and amended its constitution. The struggle for black golfers was hardly over, but the most visible symbol of the game's official prejudice against nonwhite players was finally gone.

When Tiger Woods was born, in 1975, the Caucasian-only clause was no more distant in time than the stock market crash of 1987 is from today—and the mind-set that had fostered it was very much a part of the culture of golf. One winter in the early 1970s, when I was in high school, someone from the Midwestern country club that my parents belonged to asked me to suggest some other young people who might be invited to the club's upcoming Christmas dance. I asked what would happen if my list included the names of any of the three black members of my high school class. Shortly afterward, the dance was canceled.

Golf in America is more inclusive than it was thirty years ago, but it remains conceptually inseparable from the country club, one of our least noble cultural innovations. In Great Britain, where golf was born, the game has a less disquieting heritage. Golf courses there weren't "built" in the modern sense; they evolved as players played them, and the game evolved with them. The turf was already there, and the starving livestock and the foul weather kept it relatively short. Even today, the cost of maintaining a course almost anywhere in the British Isles is usually a fraction of the cost of maintaining a course almost anywhere in the United States. In Scotland, golf began as a game of ordinary people, and for the most part it has remained a game of ordinary people; a traveling nobody with a few pounds and a handicap card can still get a game on almost any course where the British Open is played. In the early 1990s, I showed up without a tee time at Carnoustie (where the British Open was held most recently in 1999) and played two rounds for a total of less than twenty dollars; the following year, playing a single round at Pebble Beach (where the U.S. Open was held most recently in 2000) cost me close to a thousand dollars—including my green fee, my caddie's fee, and the cost of an obligatory stay at the resort. And Pebble Beach is one of just three contemporary U.S. Open venues that are in any sense public courses. (The other two are Pinehurst No. 2, where the Open was held in 1999, and the Black Course at Bethpage State Park, on Long Island, where the Open will be held in 2002.)

Golf arrived in America from Great Britain in the late 1800s and almost immediately it followed a different evolutionary path. Because the climate and terrain were so different, golf in the United States required actual real estate, as well as conscientious (and therefore expensive) upkeep. The high costs helped make American golf a game mainly of the economically privileged, and it quickly divided itself into public and private realms in a way that it never really did in Great Britain. In America, golf quickly came to embody, and thereby to aggravate, the deepest divisions in our society. It became one of the many instruments by which we subvert our theoretical dedication to equality.

Less than nine months before Woods's birth, Lee Elder became the first black golfer to qualify for an invitation to the Masters. Elder's appearance in Augusta has been celebrated ever since as an early milestone in the drearily slow enlightenment of white Americans, but it did not herald a new generation of black golfers. Like most of the few other black tour players of that time, Elder was a veteran of the old United Golfers Association, which was golf's equivalent of the Negro Leagues, and his athletic prime was mostly behind him. (He was already forty-one.) A black player named Calvin Peete, who was born in 1943 and took up golf too late to have been involved with the UGA, became one of the most prominent players on the PGA Tour in the 1980s, a decade during which he won more tournaments (eleven) than any player except Tom Kite. But Peete was virtually the end of the line. In the past twenty years, only one African-American golfer has won a PGA Tour card by way of the tour's qualifying "school." That was a now forgotten player named Adrian Stills, who qualified in 1985. "We're a dying breed," Lee Elder said last year.

Why did the black presence on tour shrink to the vanishing point between the mid-1970s and the mid-1990s, just when one would have expected the opposite? Pete McDaniel—the author of *Uneven Lies,* an illustrated cultural history of black golf in America—says, "It was the golf cart. The rise of the motorized golf cart marked the beginning of the end of minority golf, especially among African-Americans, because golf clubs that had carts didn't need caddies, and most of the black professional players had come from the caddie ranks." Golf carts, in addition to being a typically American response to the threat of mild physical exercise, eliminated what golf clubs saw as the unappealing necessity of maintaining on their premises large pools of mostly young, mostly disadvantaged workers. Carts also quickly became a cash cow, since the fees golfers paid to rent them went straight to the club. (Most fancy resort courses nowadays don't even allow players to walk, because cart rental fees are too important to the resorts' bottom line; Pebble Beach permits walkers but charges them for carts regardless.) As carts displaced caddies, kids whose families were excluded from private clubs lost their principal avenue of access to the game.

Golf may have the longest, flattest learning curve in sports. The game often promotes symptoms similar to those of obsessive-compulsive disorder, but a single exposure is seldom sufficient to establish the disease. (Becoming even a crummy player can take years.) For youngsters from the wrong side of the tracks, caddying provided the kind of gradually enticing introduction to the game that wealthy fathers had long provided for their sons and daughters. The former black touring pro Pete Brown—who began caddying when he was eleven and first played golf by sneaking onto the course where he worked, using golf clubs surreptitiously lifted from the bags of members—told McDaniel, "I watched those guys and they were so intense. A guy could play so bad one day and hit one good shot and that would make his day. He'd be back the next day. That intrigued me." When caddie programs vanished, such moments vanished with them.

Of course, a world in which a handful of black men managed to claw their way into mostly marginal professional careers as a result of having lugged the weekend baggage of wealthy whites was hardly a utopia. The real problem with golf in America, as far as race is concerned, is not that caddying declined as an occupation but that the game, over the course of more than a century, has only grudgingly made room for more than a privileged few. Given the inexorability of the cultural forces at work, it is almost unbelievable that Tiger Woods emerged as a golfer at all, much less as a golfer who has a decent chance of becoming the greatest of all time. As Earl says, Tiger is the first "naturally born and bred black professional golfer"—the first whose initial exposure to the game did not come through the service entrance. For Woods simply to have earned a Tour card and kept it for a couple of years would have made him a pioneer; doing what he has actually done moves him into the category of myth.

◦   ◦   ◦

WOODS'S OWN VIEWS about race are attractively complicated. He dislikes being referred to as "African-American," because he views that term as an insult to his mother—and so does his mother—who, after all, is Asian. Earl's ancestors were black, white, American Indian, and Asian, and Tiger has sometimes referred to his own ethnicity as "Calblinasian," a word he made up in an effort to convey most of the diversity of his genealogy. He often seems inclined to concentrate on golf and to let American race relations look after themselves, but he has invested a great deal of his increasingly scarce and valuable time in reaching out to disadvantaged children through his clinics.

Woods has been conducting clinics for young golfers since he was in high school, when he and Earl set up exhibitions in cities where Woods was playing in tournaments. The clinics ended when Woods was at Stanford, because the National Collegiate Athletic Association held that conducting them was a violation of a rule concerning individual college athletes and public exhibitions. (Earl and Tiger had several battles with the NCAA during Tiger's two years in college, and Earl says those disputes contributed to Tiger's decision to turn pro.) After Tiger left the aegis of the NCAA, late in 1996, he and Earl established the Tiger Woods Foundation to continue the mission they had begun earlier.

The Tiger Woods Foundation has been accused by

some of creating unrealistic expectations among children who have limited opportunities to become even recreational golfers, and virtually no chance at all of becoming touring pros. ("You wonder if it's false hope," a skeptical sportswriter said to me.) What good does it do—the critics have asked—to introduce an inner-city kid to a game that, for all practical purposes, can't be played in an inner city? And, indeed, if the goal is to turn more members of ethnic minorities into golfers, a simpler approach might be to concentrate directly on transforming ghetto youngsters into middle-aged Republicans—the kind of people who seem to take up the game as a matter of course. There's a public service commercial on television which shows a black child using a hammer to drive a tee into the pavement on a dark urban street, so he can tee off in his neighborhood. Well, exactly.

But there's more to it than that. Although it's true that playing on the Tour is an unreasonable ambition for almost everyone—the PGA Tour has only a hundred and twenty-five fully exempt playing spots, and many of those are held by golfers whose careers will ultimately be measured in decades rather than in years—earning a different kind of living in the world of golf is within reach for many. Unlike most other spectator sports, golf is played by millions of nonprofessionals, whose needs are served by a large industry that comprises equipment manufacturers, clothing retailers, agronomists, golf course maintenance workers, traveling salespeople, teaching professionals, scuba-diving golf ball recyclers, and others—even journalists. Within that industry, there is now a widespread conviction that if golf is to grow significantly as an economic enterprise it needs to extend its reach far beyond white suburban males. For the many Americans who don't fit that description, there has never been a better time to be looking (or training) for golf-related employment. Woods's foundation, in connection with its clinics and exhibitions, conducts seminars for children and parents in which such job opportunities are described and explained. Woods himself has estimated that as many as five percent of the children who pass through his foundation's programs will someday end up in jobs somehow connected with golf. That seems like a lot, but who knows?

Even for kids with no interest in golf-related careers, the game as a pastime has virtues that its more grotesque attributes have often obscured. Golf has a work ethic (the driving range and the practice green), a dress code (no jeans or T-shirts), and a tradition of etiquette based on personal responsibility and consideration for others (replace your divots). Spectator behavior that is tolerated and even encouraged in other sports—the frantic waving of white plastic foam tubes in an effort to fluster free throw shooters in basketball games, for example—would be considered grounds for arrest at golf tournaments, where fans are expected to keep even their shadows under control. Aspiring golfers who set out to be just like Tiger Woods may never make it to the tour, but they will inevitably end up learning something about what it takes to find and keep a job more demanding than that of filling orders at a drive-through window.

"Golf is a game in which children learn about life," Earl says. "It prepares them for life because golf is a microcosm of life. The first thing they learn is to play by the rules, and we have a lot of knuckleheads in prison today who never learned to play by the rules, because in society the rules are called laws. When children learn to play by the rules, they also learn to live their lives within the laws. They learn how to handle pressure, how to handle success, how to handle failure. Integrity, patience, honesty, discipline, you name it—they are all right there for the kids to absorb. And that makes their lives better, and it makes them better people."

Bill Dickey, who is the founder and president of a charitable foundation called the National Minority Junior Golf Scholarship Association, adds, "What Tiger is really trying to do is to help youngsters be better youngsters. And he's not doing it just because it looks good on paper." Dickey started his foundation in 1984. Operating on the thinnest of shoestrings, and living off his savings from a career in insurance and real estate, he has helped hundreds of young members of minority groups get to college and stay there. Last winter, the United States Golf Association honored him with the Joseph C. Dey Award, which is given annually "in recognition of meritorious service to the game as a volunteer." His achievement seems all the more impressive when you consider that during most of his foundation's existence, minority role models in the golf world were vanishingly scarce. Woods has changed that, too.

"Kids look at Tiger and say, 'Hey, maybe there's an opportunity for me to do that,' " Dickey says. "Now, that may be far-fetched. The game of golf is tough, and it's tougher, really, than most of the other sports. But just to have Tiger put his hand on your shoulder, if you're fortunate enough to be in a clinic with him, could have an impact on the rest of your life. Kids feel inspired because of his color—because they know he's not the traditional golf hero. And then, if they stay interested in the game, golf keeps them on kind of a good path. They learn good things about character, and about honesty, and about life."

White golfers tend to underestimate the emotional impact that Woods's racial background has on non-Caucasians. For upper-middle-class white fans, a big part of Woods's appeal is that he seems to negate racial issues altogether—he's just Tiger, the best golfer in the world. I've seen sixty-year-old white chief executive officers with their own personal jets who were as excited as a ten-year-old kid would be about having a chance to see Woods in person. Their excitement was genuine, and, to the extent that such a thing is possible, it was color-blind. When white golfers do think about Woods's racial background, it's often with a sense of relief: his dominance feels like an act of forgiveness, as though in a single spectacular career he could make up for the game's ugly past all by himself.

For many of the young players I saw in Oklahoma, though, Woods's appeal had everything to do with race: the color of his skin was the bridge they were crossing into the game. Dennis Burns, who works for the Tiger Woods Foundation and is one of a small handful of black American golf professionals (the kind who give lessons and work at golf clubs rather than play on the Tour), says, "Kids walk away from Tiger's clinics with a sense that here's a guy who looks like me and has done it. It's a feeling of confidence—and it doesn't just have to do with golf. He inspires them to do well and be great in whatever it is that they want to do." Children in general admire great athletes for most of the same reasons they admire cartoon superheroes: the constraints of the adult-ruled world don't seem to apply to them. But for teenagers who are outside America's cultural mainstream, Woods has meant incalculably more. He is the fearless conqueror of a world that has never wanted anything to do with them.

° ° °

A LESSON IN FEARLESSNESS may be what professional golfers need as well. Woods has upended their universe. Ernie Els finished second to him four times in 2000, twice in major tournaments. Els is one of the nicest people on any golf tour—and he has made nothing but generous, flabbergasted remarks about Woods—but surely it must have occurred to him that if Woods had spent four years at Stanford and then gone to graduate school, he himself might today be considered the best player in the world. He and the other young golfers who used to contend for that position, including Phil Mickelson and David Duval, have to wonder if their moment in golf history passed before it arrived. Shortly after the 2001 Masters, Duval, who had just finished in second place, two strokes behind Woods, told the sportswriter Melanie Hauser, with a note of exasperation in his voice, "I've played well enough at this point to be a four-time defending champion, or at least have won three out of the four years. I've been right there." Beginning in 1998, Duval has held or shared the lead in the Masters on numerous occasions but finished tied for second, tied for sixth, tied for third, and in second alone. What else could he do? Ahead of him lay at least a few more months of enduring sportswriters' speculation (during weeks when Woods wasn't playing somewhere) about whether he or Mickelson was the best American player who had not yet won a major.

For players who aren't Tiger Woods, there simply aren't as many major tournaments as there used to be. If Woods wins two of them each year—a possibly conservative estimate of his annual odds—that leaves just two for everybody else. Good players who are still looking for their first major victory can only worry that their opportunities are running out.

No one has to wonder where Woods ranks among all the black players who have ever played the game; as Earl has said, Tiger became the best black player in history at some point in high school, and he has never looked back. The only question remaining is whether he or Nicklaus will ultimately be regarded as the best player of all time.

Comparing athletes of different eras is treacherous, of course, although it's also irresistible. The great Bobby Jones—who remains the only player ever to have won all four of golf's major championships in a single year (although the four that he won, in 1930, were not the same four that are considered to be the majors today)—once famously observed that all an athlete can do is beat the fellows who are around when he is. He was clearly right about that. Equipment evolves, playing conditions change, and the ambitions and expectations of the players themselves cannot be extricated from the times in which they live. In Jones's day, no golfer made a living from tournament purses; all the great players, whether amateurs (like Jones) or professionals (like Harry Vardon), necessarily spent most of their time and energy doing something else—going to school and practicing law in Jones's case, conducting exhibitions in Vardon's. If Jones had been born seventy-five years later, he might have devoted himself exclusively to the game and managed to surpass his own remarkable achievements. Or he might have been overwhelmed by the depth of talent in the modern professional tour and given up, or he might never have picked up a club. Who knows?

Despite the impossibility of making comparisons across generations, in the 1970s and 1980s a growing number of sportswriters and golf fans began to believe that there had never been, and in all likelihood would never be, a better golfer than Jack Nicklaus. Nicklaus's tournament record—two United States Amateur championships, eighteen professional major championships, seventy victories on the PGA Tour—seemed staggeringly insurmountable. Various younger golfers over the years were dubbed the "Bear Apparent" (Nicklaus's nickname is "the Golden Bear"), but the bestowing of that title wound up marking the end of a promising career as often as it marked the beginning, because as soon as a golfer is tapped as a possible inheritor, his burden is increased by the considerable weight of Nicklaus's record. The player who came closest, at least for a little while, was probably Tom Watson, who is ten years younger than Nicklaus and who for several years in the late 1970s and early 1980s dominated the PGA Tour much as Nicklaus had in his prime, even beating Nicklaus head-to-head in three epic major-tournament confrontations (at the Masters and the British Open in 1977, and at the U.S. Open in 1982).

But Watson's career statistics merely underscore the monumental quality of Nicklaus's accomplishments. When Watson turned fifty, in 1999, and retired to the Senior PGA Tour, his record stood at eight major victories and thirty-four PGA Tour wins overall. In other words, as good as Watson was, he still hadn't made it halfway to Nicklaus.

Nicklaus himself identified Greg Norman, early in Norman's career, as a player with the potential to challenge his own place in the game. But Norman's career, even more than Watson's, proves that the closer a player climbs toward the summit that Nicklaus established, the thinner the air becomes. Norman's place in the game today is defined as much by tournaments he lost as it is by tournaments he won, and each of his numerous and sometimes unlucky catastrophes added to the considerable load already resting on his shoulders. As the 1996 Masters was slipping away from him, his composure must have been further eroded by his suspicion that golf fans and sportswriters and television commentators all over the world were making downward revisions in their assessments of his permanent place in the game.

But Woods so far has seemed immune to such doubts, and his icy equanimity has been a major element of his appeal. Superb athletes fascinate in part because they seem like proxies for ourselves in a metaphorical battle with the eternal: broken records are death-negating acts. Even Woods's most lopsided victories have been thrilling to watch, because his efforts have seemed so effortless—as though he had found a way to win the game that can't be won.

Will we feel the same way five years from now if no player has stepped forward to challenge him? Nicklaus had the considerable advantage during his career of being chased and, not infrequently, elbowed aside by other great players, among them Arnold Palmer, Billy Casper, Gary Player, Lee Trevino, and Tom Watson. Woods's principal adversary, so far, has been the record book. (Asked last spring whether he wished he had a close rival, Woods replied, "No, I like it the way it is.") Mickelson and Duval and Love and a handful of others occasionally step forward impressively at important moments, but you get the feeling, increasingly, that Woods has deep reserves of talent that he hasn't tapped yet, and that he will always appear to his rivals to be a receding target. If that doesn't change, then those of us who can only watch—sports fans, television commentators, sports reporters—may someday come to view his triumphs with the same dispassion that he seems to feel toward us, until the passage of time erodes his powers and makes it all seem like a contest again.

ABOUT THE AUTHOR

DAVID OWEN is a staff writer for *The New Yorker* and a contributing editor of *Golf Digest*. He is the author of eight previous books (among them *High School, The Walls Around Us, My Usual Game,* and *The Making of the Masters*). He lives in northwest Connecticut with his wife and their two children.

Printed in the United States
By Bookmasters